Evaluation of the Networks for School Improvement Initiative

Networks and Intermediaries

INTERIM REPORT

Rebecca Herman, Karen Christianson, Peter Nguyen, Susan Bush-Mecenas, Joy S. Moini, Samantha E. DiNicola, Stephani L. Wrabel, Eupha Jeanne Daramola, Pierrce Holmes, Nazia Wolters, Beth C. Gamse, Nadirah Farah Foley, Ramy Abbady, L'Heureux Lewis McCoy, Sarah Zelazny

Sponsored by the Bill & Melinda Gates Foundation

RAND EDUCATION AND LABOR

For more information on this publication, visit **www.rand.org/t/RRA242-1**.

Published by the RAND Corporation, Santa Monica, Calif.
RAND® is a registered trademark.

Library of Congress Cataloging-in-Publication Data is available for this publication.

ISBN: 978-1-9774-1317-8

Cover photo: gorodenkoff/iStock by Getty Images

About This Report

The Bill & Melinda Gates Foundation awarded five-year grants to intermediary organizations to develop networks of schools that work together using continuous improvement (CI) processes to improve educational outcomes for students who are Black, Latino, or experiencing poverty. RAND researchers are leading a study on 25 of these networks to understand how networks launch and operate and the factors that contribute to strong networks.

This report, along with a companion report that details the data sources and methodology (DiNicola, Herman, and Wrabel, 2024), summarizes findings from school years 2020–21 through 2022–23. It is a snapshot of network development; depending on when a network was funded, the networks would be in their third, fourth, or fifth year of implementation. This report is designed to help organizations that are working to improve schools, such as intermediaries and school districts, weigh strategies to use CI networks as part of their efforts. The report addresses the following research questions (RQs):

- **RQ1a:** How do intermediaries design and implement school improvement networks intended to improve the educational outcomes of Black and Latino students and students experiencing poverty?
- **RQ1b:** How and under what conditions do networks and intermediaries evolve over time?
- **RQ1c:** What intermediary strategies and contexts are associated with more-cohesive networks?

RAND Education and Labor

This study was undertaken by RAND Education and Labor, a division of RAND that conducts research on early childhood through postsecondary education programs, workforce development, and programs and policies affecting workers, entrepreneurship, and financial literacy and decisionmaking. This publication is based on research funded by the Bill & Melinda Gates Foundation. The findings and conclusions contained within are those of the authors and do not necessarily reflect positions or policies of the Bill & Melinda Gates Foundation. The foundation created the Networks for School Improvement (NSI) initiative to fund and develop networks of schools working together to improve educational outcomes for students who are Black, Latino, or experiencing poverty. For more information on this and other related topics, please visit www.gatesfoundation.org.

More information about RAND can be found at www.rand.org. Questions about this report should be directed to Becki Herman at bherman@rand.org, and questions about RAND Education and Labor should be directed to educationandlabor@rand.org.

Acknowledgments

We are grateful to the intermediary, network, and district staff who participated in our annual data collection activities over the past three years. Their time and willingness to share information about their work and perspectives on the NSI initiative made this work possible. We thank Tiffany Berglund for her work on the Team Connections Survey administration and analysis. We also thank the team who coded the scores of interview and focus group transcripts, which made the analysis possible. We thank Maxwell Yurkofsky (Radford University), Alice Huguet (RAND), and Benjamin Master (RAND), our quality-assurance reviewers, for helpful feedback that improved this report. Finally, we would like to thank the Bill & Melinda Gates Foundation for its support of this work and Andy Sokatch for his guidance and leadership of the evaluation effort overall. Thanks also to Vivian Mihalakis, Susan Fairchild, and Katherine Martin of the Bill & Melinda Gates Foundation for sharing background and insights on the NSI work. We are also grateful for the collaboration with our evaluation partners at AIR, Mathematica, MDRC, and Abt Associates.

Summary

The Bill & Melinda Gates Foundation established the Networks for School Improvement (NSI) initiative to support networks of schools in using continuous improvement (CI) processes to improve outcomes for students who are Black, Latino, or experiencing poverty. Each network involves an *intermediary*—a central organization that facilitates the network and supports schools (e.g., a technical assistance provider or school district)—and school-specific CI teams of staff (e.g., teachers, school leaders) that guide change initiatives in their schools. RAND researchers are leading a study on 25 of these networks to understand how networks launch and operate and the factors that contribute to strong networks (Research Question 1 [RQ1]). The American Institutes for Research (AIR) is leading a concurrent study on school implementation of CI activities (RQ2), and Mathematica is leading a study on the impact of these networks on student outcomes (RQ3). The suite of reports is available at www.rand.org/nsi.

This report summarizes findings about the networks from school years 2020–21, 2021–22, and 2022–23. It presents a snapshot of network development; depending on when each network was funded, the report covers the third, fourth, or fifth year of implementation. The report addresses the following questions:

- **RQ1a:** How do intermediaries design and implement school improvement networks intended to improve the educational outcomes of Black and Latino students and students experiencing poverty?
- **RQ1b:** How and under what conditions do networks and intermediaries evolve over time?
- **RQ1c:** What intermediary strategies and contexts are associated with more-cohesive networks?

In this report, we first describe the common models and strategies that are in place across these intermediaries to create and lead their networks, facilitate learning among network members, and help build schools' capacity to use CI to improve outcomes for students who are Black, Latino, or experiencing poverty. Then, we explore crosscutting patterns in how the networks and intermediaries sought to center equity in these activities and how network activities shifted over time. We conclude by examining patterns in network engagement and development of network cohesiveness.

First, we found that intermediaries combined centralized leadership with local adaptation to organize and build the capacity of their networks. During the design and network creation phase, intermediaries tapped their existing relationships with schools and districts to build their membership and critically assessed potential members before inviting them to join. Generally, intermediaries led the network formation—including establishing network goals—and made efforts to incorporate the priorities of member schools. Intermediaries actively supported members in sharing CI strategies across the network, mainly through regular convenings but also through smaller meetings and knowledge management systems. They primarily used coaching to help network members build capacity for CI and actively supported members in gathering and making sense of data.

Second, we found that intermediaries sought to center equity across these activities. Intermediaries worked to improve their own organizational knowledge of racial, ethnic, and socioeconomic inequalities by providing learning experiences for staff and embedding equity into core organizational practices (e.g., staffing assignments). They also supported CI teams in promoting equity, most commonly through disaggregating student data to identify gaps in achievement and help focus efforts on reducing those gaps.

Third, we observed changes in how intermediaries approached capacity-building and network facilitation over time. The NSI aimed to engage participants in joint work and increase empowerment of CI teams. In particular, we saw shifts in the following areas: increasing the focus on equity, shifting leadership from the intermediary to CI teams, and adjusting CI activities to the local context.

Finally, we explored the relationship between *network cohesion*—a measure of the extent to which members of a network are connected—and network strategies because a positive relationship between network cohesion and network effectiveness has been found in prior research (e.g., an unpublished 2020 review by RAND researchers Susan Bush-Mecenas, Karen Christianson, Andrea Prado Tuma, Grace Gahlon, Monica Rico, and Ivy Todd). Networks that were especially cohesive appeared to use common strategies: They tended to host recurring role-alike meetings, create cross-school small discussion groups, ask specific schools to present on their work to the rest of the network, and facilitate cross-school site visits.

Using our theoretical framework, we anticipated that the nature of the networks and intermediaries, how far along they were in implementation, and the district context could influence NSI activities. In exploratory analysis,[1] we found few clear trends, and those that we did find were disparate and hard to explain. Overall, we found that cohort and entry point largely did not shape changes in how intermediaries approached the NSI work over time.[2] This finding may be related to intermediaries' use of a common model (e.g., Bryk, Gomez, and Grunow, 2011), which drove networks toward similar approaches regardless of their differences. Furthermore, throughout the grant period, the networks were embedded in a programwide community of practice and perhaps learned from and mirrored each other in real time, regardless of cohort and entry point. Alternatively, powerful changes in context (e.g., the coronavirus disease 2019 pandemic, school closures) may have shaped the choices of networks, overshadowing more subtle distinctions among them. We will continue to explore these patterns—and their impact on student outcomes—in the final report.

---

[1] The exploratory analysis focused only on explaining practices that changed over time. The analysis in the final report will examine all practices, regardless of whether they changed over time.

[2] The foundation categorized the networks into three entry points based on their aim statements and change ideas: *instructional* (working to improve the quality of instruction within classrooms), *early warning and response* (working to create more-supportive, connected school environments), and *well-matched postsecondary* (working to support postsecondary application, enrollment, and persistence).

Contents

Figures and Tables

Figures

Tables

CHAPTER 1

Background on the Networks for School Improvement Initiative and Evaluation

The Networks for School Improvement Initiative

The Bill & Melinda Gates Foundation (the foundation) established the Networks for School Improvement (NSI) to increase the proportion of Black students, Latino students, and students experiencing poverty who are on track for high school graduation and college enrollment.[1] The initiative supports networks of schools in using continuous improvement (CI) methods to identify and test strategies designed to improve teachers' practices and student supports. Each NSI consists of an intermediary organization leading a network of about 20 schools (ranging from fewer than 10 to more than 50 schools) and supporting teams of school staff in conducting CI. These intermediaries have partnered with almost 800 schools across approximately 150 districts and charter networks to identify, test, refine, and scale strategies to improve students' academic and behavioral outcomes.

The foundation funded three cohorts of five-year grants between 2018 and 2020, totaling more than $300 million in funding (see Table 1.1).[2] Most intermediaries leading NSI are nonprofit education organizations and university-affiliated centers; three are school districts and one is a charter school network (see the appendix for a full list of NSI grantees). Each NSI focused its grant on improving student outcomes in one or more of the following areas:

- **8th- or 9th-grade on track:** The proportion of 8th- or 9th-grade students who meet a set of academic and behavioral outcomes related to high school graduation and college enrollment
- **College-ready on track:** The proportion of 11th- and 12th-grade students who are on track academically to enroll in a college with a graduation rate of at least 50 percent
- **Well-matched postsecondary enrollment:** The proportion of 12th-grade students who complete the steps needed to enroll in a college with a graduation rate of at least 50 percent.

The foundation also categorized each NSI in one of three "entry points" based on the primary focus of their CI activities: *instructional* (working to improve the quality of instruction within classrooms), *early warning and response* (working to create more supportive, connected school environments), and *well-matched postsecondary* (working to support postsecondary application, enrollment, and persistence). Entry points are similar but not identical to outcome areas. For example, an NSI that aims to improve college-ready on-track

[1] We use the term *Latino* to refer to peoples of Latin American descent. While we acknowledge the use of *Latinx* to indicate gender inclusivity, we also understand that *Latinx* and other iterations (e.g., *Latin@*, *Latine*) may not be accepted by those from Latin American communities (Salinas, 2020). Given this context, we use *Latino* because it is generally embraced by the communities that are reflected in this work without violating their sociolinguistic norms.

[2] The foundation awarded 31 grants to intermediary organizations that funded 34 individual networks. One intermediary received a single grant that funded four networks.

TABLE 1.1
NSI Grant Years, by Cohort

Cohort	2018–19 School Year	2019–20 School Year	2020–21 School Year	2021–22 School Year	2022–23 School Year
1	Year 1	Year 2	Year 3	Year 4	Year 5
1B/2		Year 1	Year 2	Year 3	Year 4
3			Year 1	Year 2	Year 3

outcomes might use an instructional entry point or early warning and response entry point to achieve that outcome.

The NSI partnered with large, mostly urban districts that served a higher proportion of students who are Black, Latino, or experiencing poverty, compared to districts nationally (Figure 1.1). The median enrollment of districts with NSI schools was 13,000 students, compared to 1,000 for districts nationally. In addition, the NSI districts had more than double the percentage of Latino students and students attending high-poverty schools than districts nationally.

The coronavirus disease 2019 (COVID-19) pandemic affected the work of all three cohorts of NSI grants. The first two NSI cohorts had already commenced at the onset of the pandemic in spring 2020, and the pandemic delayed the start of Cohort 3 in fall 2020 by six to nine months. After shifting to virtual instruction in spring 2020, NSI districts provided in-person instruction for about a third of the 2020–21 school year, on average. NSI adapted their grant activities to help educators respond to pandemic-related disruptions and the challenges of virtual instruction. The disruptions to schooling during this period contributed to lost learning opportunities and larger achievement gaps (Fahle et al., 2023; Goldhaber et al., 2022; Jack et al., 2023). Although schools returned to in-person instruction in the 2021–22 school year, they continued to face challenges with chronic absenteeism, student mental health, and academic recovery (Cattan et al., 2023; Dee, 2024; Liu, Lee, and Gershenson, 2021).

The NSI Evaluation

The foundation sponsored an evaluation to build evidence on the NSI approach. Despite growing efforts to support school networks in using CI to test and refine solutions to educational challenges, there is limited evidence on the implementation and impact (Feygin et al., 2020). In particular, there is little evidence on the characteristics of effective school networks (according to an unpublished 2020 review by RAND researchers Susan Bush-Mecenas, Karen Christianson, Andrea Prado Tuma, Grace Gahlon, Monica Rico, and Ivy Todd), and there are few studies on the use of CI in education settings (Garet et al., 2021). The NSI initiative provides a valuable opportunity to address these evidence gaps and learn about the formation of school networks, the use of CI in schools, and the impact of these efforts on student outcomes. The evaluation addresses three main research questions:

1. How do intermediaries design and implement their NSI?
2. To what extent do participating schools implement CI activities?
3. What is the impact of the NSI on student outcomes? What aspects of the NSI approach are related to impacts on students?

Each research question is addressed by a different evaluation partner: RAND leads work on Research Question 1 (RQ1), the American Institutes for Research (AIR) leads work on Research Question 2 (RQ2),

FIGURE 1.1
Characteristics of Districts with NSI Schools in the Evaluation, Compared to Districts Nationwide

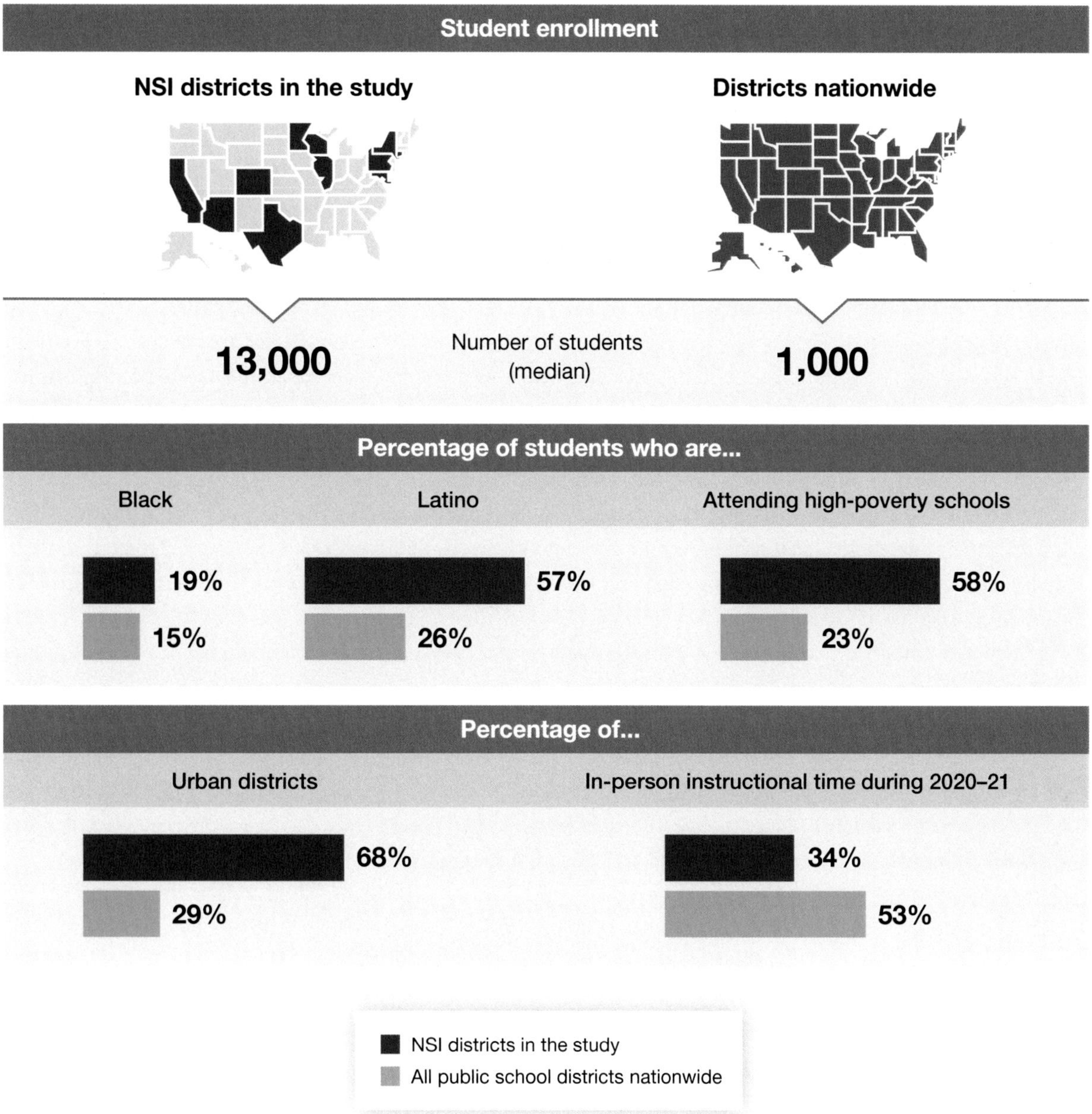

SOURCES: Features data from American Enterprise Institute, undated; U.S. Department of Education, undated.
NOTE: The figure shows average district characteristics weighted by the number of students in NSI schools (NSI districts) or by the number of students in the district (districts nationwide). *High-poverty schools* are defined as schools with at least 75 percent of students eligible for free or reduced-price lunch.

and Mathematica leads work on Research Question 3 (RQ3). The first set of evaluation reports (interim reports) describes implementation of the NSI through the 2022–23 school year (RQ1 and RQ2) and impacts on student outcomes through the 2021–22 school year (RQ3). A second set of reports (final reports) in 2026 will describe two more school years of NSI implementation and impacts. This report and its companion report (DiNicola, Herman, and Wrabel, 2024) present findings on RQ1. The suite of reports is available at www.rand.org/nsi.

The findings in this report are preliminary because the analysis of implementation is based on the third year of the evaluation, which is the third, fourth, or fifth year of implementation (depending on when the grant was awarded). The evaluation will ultimately look at all five years of implementation and, for some NSI, a year of sustained effort after the end of the grant. The additional data will facilitate better analysis of patterns over time. In addition, the later analysis will be better positioned to differentiate patterns related to NSI implementation from those that may have been affected by the COVID-19 pandemic.

The NSI Initiative's Conceptual Framework

The foundation outlined a broad structure for NSI while also providing flexibility for intermediaries to adapt their approach. The evaluation teams developed a conceptual framework to describe the key features of the NSI approach and guide the evaluation (Figure 1.2). According to this framework, intermediaries create and support networks of schools in using CI to improve practices related to their outcome area (Figure 1.2, panel A). The NSI initiative—at the intermediary, network, and school levels—centers equity to ensure schools focus on improving outcomes for students who are Black, Latino, or experiencing poverty.[3] Schools in the network form teams of teachers, counselors, administrators, and other staff (called *CI teams*) to participate in the NSI (Figure 1.2, panel B). Intermediaries provide coaching and professional learning to school CI teams to develop their capacity to engage in meaningful CI processes. Intermediaries also provide additional supports to the CI teams that generally include the data to understand the challenge, a knowledge management system to document what CI teams learn, and network convenings to strengthen connections between teams and share learning across the network.

The foundation expects school CI teams to engage in CI processes that included the six core parameters shown in panel C of Figure 1.2. These core parameters mirror the six core principles of CI outlined by the Carnegie Foundation for the Advancement of Teaching (Bryk et al., 2015). The NSI core parameters focus on developing an understanding of the problem and its root causes; identifying a specific goal or aim for addressing the problem; describing the key factors and conditions needed to accomplish the aim (the theory of practice improvement); selecting specific strategies—called *change ideas*[4]—to achieve the aim; and using disciplined inquiry cycles and data to test and refine the change ideas.

Schools' participation in the NSI and their use of CI processes are expected to improve educators' practices and student supports and, ultimately, to improve on-track outcomes for students who are Black, Latino, or experiencing poverty (Figure 1.2, panel D).

In the long term, effective strategies identified by CI teams can be shared with other educators in participating schools and more broadly across a district or charter network (Figure 1.2, panel E). Building educators' capacity to develop and test strategies that address ongoing challenges is expected to improve the school culture.

The analysis in this report focuses on panel A of Figure 1.2, how intermediaries establish their networks and provide supports, and a portion of panel B, focused on network cohesion and supports.

---

3 The evaluation team views educational equity as providing students with resources, experiences, and environments—allocated based on circumstances and needs—so that students have equal access to opportunities for success (Thompson and Thompson, 2018).

4 See the glossary for a more detailed definition of *change ideas*.

FIGURE 1.2
NSI Conceptual Framework

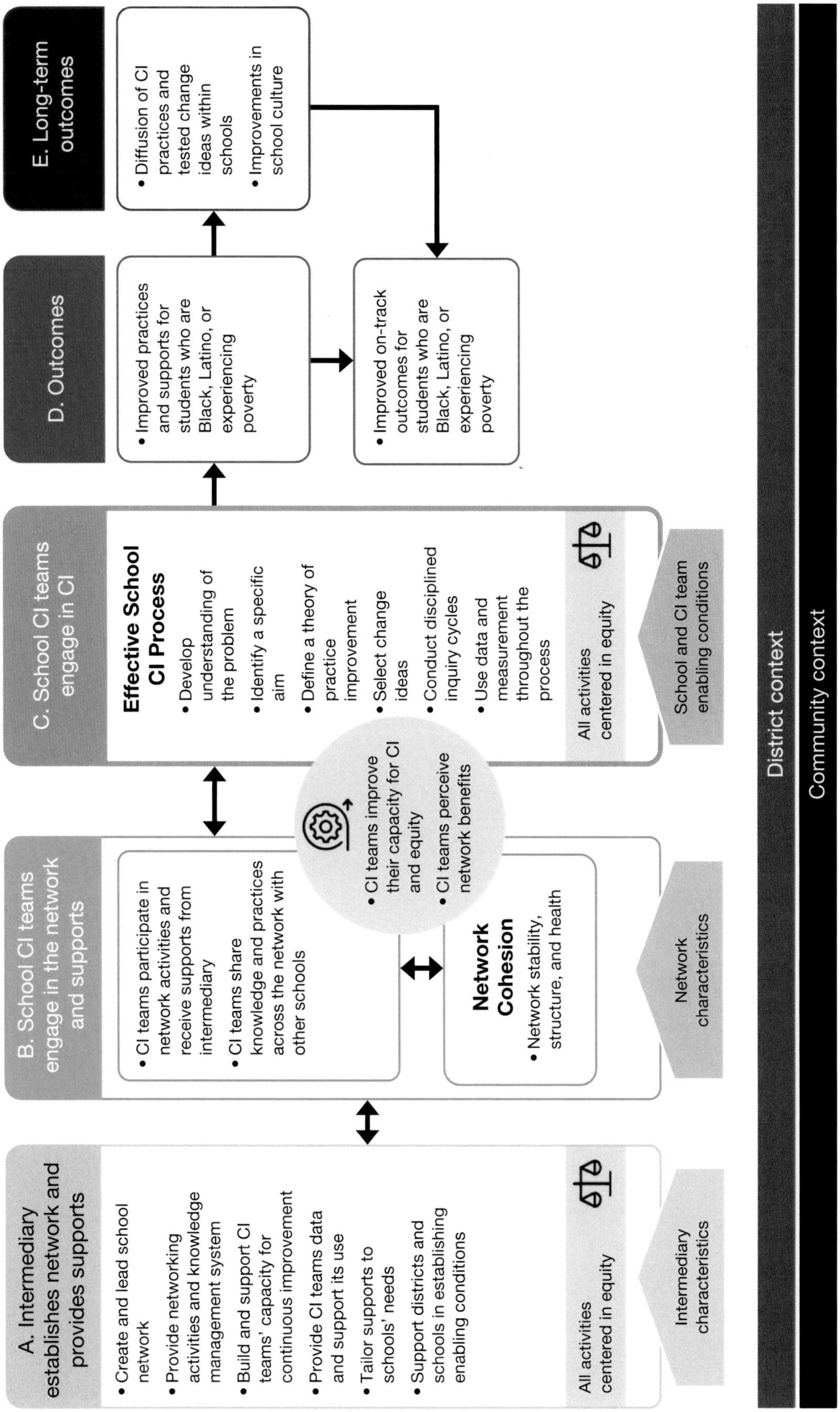

CHAPTER 2

RQ1 Study Design and Sample

The NSI initiative provides the opportunity to study an exceptionally large and diverse group of school improvement networks. Although there are studies of specific networks, there is no existing research that looks at a large group of varied school improvement networks. We anticipate that the study results will help network developers, districts, and schools consider their options and make well-informed decisions on how to best improve schools through collaboration and improvement science. This interim report describes the operation of school improvement networks, challenges in implementing such networks, and strategies for operating networks well. The final report will explore the qualities of networks and partners related to school improvement. This report addresses the following research questions:

- **RQ1a:** How do intermediaries design and implement school improvement networks intended to improve the educational outcomes of Black and Latino students and students experiencing poverty?
- **RQ1b:** How and under what conditions do networks and intermediaries evolve?
- **RQ1c:** What intermediary strategies and contexts are associated with more-cohesive networks?

Our study design and sample are briefly described in Box 2.1. A more detailed description of our methodology, including selection procedures, data collection, and data analysis, can be found in the companion report (DiNicola, Herman, and Wrabel, 2024).

BOX 2.1

RQ1 Study Design and Sample

How did we evaluate networks?

We examined the implementation of 25 NSI over three years, focusing on the work of the intermediaries that designed and led the networks, as well as the functioning of the networks themselves. Through systematic coding and analysis, we identified patterns in activities, roles and responsibilities, and relationships, both across networks and over time. We analyzed data by school year, providing a snapshot of network implementation each year.

How did we collect data?

- **Team Connections Survey:** This survey asked one self-selected representative from each CI team about their interactions with other CI teams and the intermediary organization in their network.
- **Intermediary staff interviews:** We asked network staff (i.e., leaders, coaches, equity leaders, other intermediary staff) about intermediary- and network-level activities, supports for network participants, strategies for centering equity, the role of districts and school leaders, and key enabling conditions and challenges. We attempted to conduct three interviews for each network and seven to ten interviews for each case study network.
- **CI team focus groups:** We asked case study network CI team members who volunteered for focus groups about their experiences as network participants and the enabling conditions and challenges of their work.
- **District staff interviews:** We asked district staff (from the districts in which case study networks operate) about their roles, the alignment of the network(s) with their district's work, and interactions with the intermediary.
- **Network convening observations:** We aimed to observe spring convening events for each of the five case study networks, paying close attention to the content, structure, and timing of convening activities, as well as the interactions and engagement among presenters and participants.
- **Partners for Network Improvement (PNI) Network Health Survey:** This survey asked CI team members and intermediary staff about intermediary leadership, network roles and engagement, network connections, and CI.

Which networks did we include in our sample?

In general, the sample for the study was 25 networks across Cohorts 1, 1B/2, and 3. We selected 25 of the 34 grantee networks, prioritizing those that provided sufficient schools for RQ3 analysis, aligned with the NSI's overall outcome areas, and worked with entire grade levels. We also selected five networks for case studies, aiming to maximize variation on intermediary and network characteristics and types of interventions. The table on the next page displays the number of networks represented by each data source in each year in this report. The 25 networks received funding by cohort in three waves. Therefore, networks may have been at different stages of development in any given study year. The study captured insights from some networks at the start of their NSI work (Cohort 3, grant year 1 in school year [SY] 2020–21) and others at a later point (e.g., Cohort 1, grant year 5 in SY2022–23).

BOX 2.1—CONTINUED

Number of Networks Providing Data, by Data Source and School Year

	SY2020–21 (*N* = 23)	SY2021–22 (*N* = 25)	SY2022–23 (*N* = 25)	
Data Source	**Actual Sample**	**Actual Sample**	**Actual Sample**	**Intended Sample**
Team Connections Survey	14	19	15	15
Intermediary staff interviews	23	25	25	25
Focus groups (CI team members)	4	4	4	5
District staff interviews	9	2	10	15
Network convening observations	7	4	3	5
PNI Network Health Survey	22	25	NA[a]	NA

NOTE: NA = not applicable.

[a] Data from the Spring 2023 PNI Network Health Survey are not included in this report because they were not available at the time of writing.

What limitations apply to our findings?

- Data may not fully reflect all activities, strategies, challenges, and enablers of networks. These data show a snapshot of the work at the time of data collection.
- Data reflect the perspectives of intermediary, school, and district staff, which may result in varying statements of goals or approaches within a single network.
- We report the change over time for questions that were asked in multiple years. These changes may be influenced, in part, by the variations in samples across years and the changes made to data collection protocols each year.

See the companion report for more detail (DiNicola, Herman, and Wrabel, 2024).

CHAPTER 3

Findings

The findings in this report are organized by the intermediary components of the NSI conceptual framework (see Figure 1.2) and address the following research questions:

- **RQ1a:** How do intermediaries design and implement school improvement networks intended to improve the educational outcomes of Black and Latino students and students experiencing poverty?
- **RQ1b:** How and under what conditions do networks and intermediaries evolve?
- **RQ1c:** What intermediary strategies and contexts are associated with more-cohesive networks?

To address RQ1a, we describe the common approaches, strategies, and practices that networks used as they designed and implemented networks (see Figure 1.2, panel A). To begin, we describe the steps that intermediaries took to *create and lead a network*, including recruiting schools, setting network goals, and building internal staff capacity. Next, we explain how intermediaries *provide networking activities*. We then describe how intermediaries *build and support capacity* of school staff (i.e., mostly through coaching) and, in some cases, provide supports to district staff. We conclude with a description of how intermediaries *provide and support use of data*.

We present crosscutting analyses examining the centering of equity in intermediary activities and shifts in these activities over time. We then expand on the primary strategies that intermediaries used to center equity within their networks and why this matters. To address RQ1b, we highlight patterns in how networks have *evolved*. Together, these sections illuminate how NSI established its networks and provided supports (see Figure 1.2, panel A). Finally, to address RQ1c, we share our findings on the intermediary activities and contexts associated with *network cohesion* (see Figure 1.2, panel B).

Each section includes key findings that we identified from our data.[1] These findings are presented in **bold**. We often present results by the percentage of networks for which a statement is true, based on the data we collected. Where we have multiple years of relevant data, we present findings from multiple years for all of the networks in our sample: SY2020–21, SY2021–22, and SY2022–23.

Intermediary Establishes a Network and Provides Support

Create and Lead a Network

Intermediaries used a variety of strategies and priorities in their approaches to creating and leading a network. In recruiting schools to a network, common approaches included leveraging existing relationships, using formal processes, and prioritizing equity. We also describe how intermediaries established shared network goals and developed internal staff capacity to support equity within the network.

[1] The findings about common strategies emerged from data analysis. In general, the foundation did not require intermediaries to use specific strategies. It is possible that the twice-yearly foundation-led community of practice meetings had a norming effect—practices used in one NSI or featured at the meetings might have spread to other NSI.

Recruiting Schools to a School Improvement Network

Here, we report on the priorities that guided intermediaries in recruiting schools and districts to their networks and the extent to which CI team members perceived the process for joining their network as clear. The data for this section come from the first year of this study (SY2020–21), the time when most networks were still recruiting or had recently recruited the schools for their network. Table 3.1 lists the most common recruitment strategies and priorities, which are described in more detail in the findings that follow.

Most intermediaries leveraged existing relationships to recruit schools for the network. The majority of intermediaries (83 percent) leveraged existing relationships with schools, school leaders, and district leaders to recruit schools to participate in networks. Intermediary staff from almost half of all the networks we interviewed stated that they recruited from districts where they had previously led a network. District interviewees concurred: All respondents who were able to answer the question reported having a prior relationship with the intermediary. Intermediaries tapped their relationships with districts, and, in at least one case, the district built on its relationships with schools to help bring schools to the network. As one staff member explained,

> [This district] is a very relationship-oriented type of culture . . . The [district leaders] that we have who are network chiefs have very strong relationships with their school principals. They were the ones who said basically, "I think you should do this" and just on that [relationship] alone . . . [schools] joined because of that referral.

Intermediaries used, and communicated clearly about, formal processes to purposefully select schools and districts for the network. In addition, the majority of intermediaries used formal processes to select and onboard member schools. More than half of interviewed intermediaries (52 percent) required some sort of application process to join the network. Intermediaries judged the fit of the school with the network using school characteristics (e.g., adequate staffing, stable leadership, school type, student demographics) and priorities of the school or district (e.g., a focus on equity, alignment between network and school or district goals, need for services offered by the intermediary). On the 2021 PNI Network Health Survey, participants

TABLE 3.1
Strategies and Priorities for Recruitment

Strategies and Priorities	Number of Intermediaries That Responded Affirmatively (N = 23)
Strategies	
Leveraging existing relationships	19
Using formal application processes	12
Priorities	
Alignment with NSI goals	11
Sufficient and stable staffing	8
High proportion of Black or Latino students or students experiencing poverty	7
Mix of school types	6
Local schools that have a need for NSI	5
Existing school focus on equity	4

SOURCE: Intermediary staff, interviews with authors, spring/summer of SY2020–21.

in the average network agreed—but did not strongly agree—with such statements as, "The network has a clear process for selecting new members" (3.60 average rating on a 5-point scale) or "The network communicates clear expectations for how new members will participate" (3.92 average rating on a 5-point scale).[2]

Equity was a recruitment priority for the majority of intermediaries; in turn, most networks included participants from diverse backgrounds and with equity expertise. More than half of interviewed networks (52 percent) in SY2020–21 described prioritizing equity as they recruited. They considered the school's student demographics (30 percent); whether the school had an existing equity focus, as evidenced by existing equity initiatives (17 percent); or whether the school had an identified need for support focusing on equity (22 percent) as part of their recruitment approach. The networks included members with diverse backgrounds who could bring a "lived experience" to the work. In addition, the networks included members with expertise on diversity, equity, and inclusion strategies. As shown in Table 3.2, network participants, in the average network, who responded to the 2021 PNI Network Health Survey agreed or strongly agreed that their network included people from diverse backgrounds and with expertise in diversity, equity, and inclusion.

Establishing Network Goals

By definition, school improvement networks aim to collaborate toward common goals (unpublished 2020 review by RAND researchers Susan Bush-Mecenas, Karen Christianson, Andrea Prado Tuma, Grace Gahlon, Monica Rico, and Ivy Todd), and prior research suggests that a shared mission is related to effective network functioning (Chapman and Varda, 2017; Edelenbos and Klijn, 2007; Goldsmith and Eggers, 2004; McGuire, 2006). In this section, we outline the strategies that networks used to establish shared goals among member schools, as well as the equity-focused approaches they used to work toward achieving those goals.

Intermediaries tended to involve schools in developing network goals, although some networks shifted their approach to be more top-down over time. All networks had a clearly articulated goal by SY2022–23. In most cases, networks had clearly articulated this goal as early as SY2020–21 (which was the first year of implementation for Cohort 3 but the third for Cohort 1), and that goal remained consistent in subsequent years. A small number of networks did not clearly articulate a goal in SY2020–21 but had a more clearly articulated emphasis by SY2021–22.

TABLE 3.2

Participants from Diverse Backgrounds and with Equity Expertise

The Network . . .	Average Network Rating	Standard Deviation
Has brought together a group of people with diverse backgrounds, perspectives, and expertise	4.38	0.31
Includes members with relevant diversity, equity, and inclusion expertise to inform our improvement activities	4.35	0.29
Includes diverse leaders who represent the educators and students in the schools we seek to improve	4.29	0.32

NOTE: Findings are from the 2021 PNI Network Health Survey; *N* = 22 networks. Responses were rated on a scale of 1 (do not agree) to 5 (strongly agree).

[2] Survey responses were rated on a 5-point scale, where 1 = do not agree, 2 = slightly agree, 3 = moderately agree, 4 = agree, and 5 = strongly agree.

In SY2020–21, interviewed intermediary staff described having schools create school-specific aims under the umbrella of a common goal (57 percent). One staff member explained,

> Last year, we kind of gave some boundaries, some guardrails, and said, "OK, you can do anything, but they have to fit within our Rise by Five strategies." That was good in terms of being able to then . . . cohort some of our schools with, "OK, you're focusing on this similar strategy, so you all can learn from each other here."

Intermediary staff at roughly one-third of networks (35 percent) described collaborating with schools to develop the common goal. However, intermediary staff at less than half of networks (39 percent) reported setting a common goal or aim for the network without school input.[3] Similarly, CI team members in the average network reported on the 2022 PNI Network Health Survey that most peer network participants were working toward a common goal (4.19 rating on a 5-point scale), were invested in the success of the network as a whole (4.04 rating on a 5-point scale), and were actively working toward the network's collective success (4.02 rating on a 5-point scale).[4] Although we did not ask about goal development in subsequent years, there is some evidence that intermediaries' approaches may shift as a network matures. Intermediary staff spoke about trying to calibrate the right level of "tightness" or "looseness" for the network, with some intermediaries taking a stronger, more directive lead over time, and other intermediaries allowing more autonomy at the school level in later years.

For the most part, network goals did not explicitly focus on equity. In general, network goals did not state equity as a goal. Roughly one-fourth of interviewed networks (22 percent) in SY2020–21 indicated that advancing equity was inherently part of their network goal by virtue of the network's explicit focus on marginalized populations or the demographics of the schools participating in the network. In addition, intermediary staff at roughly one-fourth of networks (22 percent) reported that their network goals lacked a clear focus on equity in SY2020–21.

Building Intermediaries' Internal Capacity to Support Equity

In this section, we describe how intermediaries build their own capacity to lead and support networks aimed at improving outcomes for Black and Latino students and students experiencing poverty. Table 3.3 lists the most common strategies that interviewed intermediaries reported using to build their capacity to center equity within their networks and intermediary organization(s).

TABLE 3.3
Strategies for Developing Intermediary Capacity to Center Equity Within the NSI

Strategy	SY2020–21 (*N* = 23)	SY2021–22 (*N* = 25)	SY2022–23 (*N* = 25)
Regular staff meetings, professional development	12	14	13
Affinity groups	7	2	3
Professional development to shift mindsets	1	6	3
Hiring	3	1	2
Activities to build trust	1	2	1

SOURCE: Intermediary staff, interviews with authors, spring/summer of each year of data collection.

[3] Some respondents within the same intermediary articulated goals or characterized approaches differently, leading a single network to be identified within multiple goal-setting categories.

[4] Response options for this 5-point scale were as follows: 1 = very few, 2 = some, 3 = about half, 4 = most, and 5 = all network members.

Intermediaries aimed to improve their staff's understanding of equity issues and strategies to address inequity through staff development and targeted hiring. In interviews, intermediary staff described using a variety of strategies to build their internal capacity to lead networks focused on equity. In SY2022–23, more than half (52 percent) described some sort of standing staff meeting or professional development session to focus on issues related to equity within the intermediary organization. Intermediary staff mentioned finding it useful to dedicate time to discuss these issues with colleagues. One staff member explained that their monthly equity-focused professional development helps make equity work more tangible:

> We have our own monthly kind of development on [race, class, culture, and power]. It's kind of like an org-wide, all-day thing. We're both closer together, and I think the opportunity to do that work within our organization at a pretty deep level . . . makes it a lot easier for us to carry out that work in schools and to have . . . concrete language and concrete examples of what we're asking leaders to do, and we're asking them to do a lot of really difficult work, and I think being able to say, . . . "We're not asking you to do something that we're also not doing ourselves," I think is really important.

While some intermediary staff valued these professional development activities, staff from a small handful of intermediaries—4 percent in SY2022–23, 12 percent in SY2021–22, and 10 percent in SY2020–21—characterized their organization's internal capacity-building activities as sporadic, infrequent, or insufficient. Other strategies reported in SY2022–23 included creating affinity groups (12 percent), particularly for White team members to learn about and process how their racial and ethnic identity shapes the work they do advancing equity for Black and Latino students, and conducting professional development activities (12 percent) aimed at changing intermediary staff mindsets. Intermediary staff at a couple of networks (8 percent) also described the importance of hiring and retaining diverse staff. Interestingly, there was substantial shifting in the most popular strategies from year to year, and many intermediaries tried different strategies at different times. For example, 13 intermediaries were using regular staff meetings to develop their capacity in SY2022–23, but 22 intermediaries had taken this approach at least once over the three-year period. Moreover, in SY2022–23, nearly one-third of networks developed a working group or committee of staff that was tasked to lead the work on capacity-building for equity.

Provide Networking Activities

In addition to working directly with individual CI teams and district staff, intermediaries also leveraged the school networks to support cross-team sharing and spread learnings across the network. We first provide an overview of the most common strategies, including the knowledge management systems used to house data, protocols, and best practice resources. Then we look closer at the most prevalent network-sharing structure—convenings—and highlight findings from observations of case study site convenings.

Network members shared change ideas, successes, CI approaches, and other work mainly through convenings and small group meetings of members with similar roles. Most commonly, intermediary staff reported using gatherings of network participants to facilitate sharing between schools (see Table 3.4). All networks in SY2022–23 hosted *convenings* (large gatherings with multiple participants from each school) on average four times per year. Convenings often included activities designed for cross-school sharing, such as having each school present a poster on a successful change idea they enacted or dividing participants into small cross-school groups to discuss what they have learned from their data. In addition to convenings, the majority of networks (72 percent) also reported hosting recurring role-alike meetings for a subset of network participants (e.g., team leaders, school leaders) with typically monthly or bimonthly opportunities for cross-school learning. Intermediaries also had coaches "disperse and pollinate ideas" between schools through either sharing learning from one school with another school (52 percent) or facilitating connections between schools

TABLE 3.4
Structures to Facilitate Network Sharing

Structure	SY2020–21 (*N* = 23)	SY2021–22 (*N* = 25)	SY2022–23 (*N* = 25)
Whole-network convenings	23	24	25
Recurring role-alike meetings	11	15	18
Coaches sharing with other schools	12	12	13
Coaches encouraging connection	14	7	8
Knowledge management systems	6	8	8
Cross-school visits	2	2	7

SOURCE: Intermediary staff, interviews with authors, spring/summer of each year of data collection.

with similar focuses (32 percent). On the SY2022–23 Team Connections Survey, the majority of respondents (75 percent) in a network agreed or strongly agreed that their coach helped connect them to other schools.

Roughly one-third of networks (32 percent) used knowledge management systems (e.g., online collaboration platform, shared drive, data dashboard) to share resources. Generally, intermediaries described using these platforms to share spotlights and successes of specific change ideas, exemplar CI resources, theories about and approaches to CI implementation, and strategies for centering equity in their work.

Networks in the NSI initiative were often more effective than the other professional networks available to school staff, according to district staff. The majority of district staff interviewees in SY2022–23 (86 percent) reported that staff in both NSI and non-NSI schools have access to other professional networks, such as grade-level teams or districtwide leadership teams. The professional networks available to non-NSI schools share some similarities with the NSI's professional networks, such as common purposes, dedicated meeting times, and cross-district convenings. Some non-NSI networks are within schools (e.g., school improvement teams), whereas networks in the NSI initiative mainly connect across schools. The majority of district staff (71 percent) indicated that the NSI function more effectively because they are more structured and consistent, have access to dedicated coaching, and provide external accountability. One district employee also noted that the CI team participating in the NSI is higher-functioning than other non-NSI CI teams. She explained,

> Every school and every department has a PLC [professional learning community]. What's different is you'll find a spectrum of highly functioning PLCs to very dysfunctional PLCs and somewhere in the middle. [Our NSI network school] has . . . the highest, one of the highest-functioning PLCs I've ever seen. If I were to create the spectrum so we can measure of what a highly effective PLC looks like, the [School] Middle Math Department would be the model I would love to see scaled and replicated.

Networks used convenings to share progress, develop CI team members' knowledge and skills, and plan future work; nearly half of the intermediaries dedicated time to discuss equity. Most commonly, intermediaries used convening time to have CI teams share progress on their CI initiatives and experiences with the implementation of change ideas (80 percent of networks in SY2022–23, similar to prior years). These sessions centered on sharing experiences and learning, reflecting on successes and challenges, and getting feedback from peers (see Figure 3.1).

Almost half of networks (48 percent) reported addressing equity in their convenings in SY2022–23. Intermediary staff at 16 percent of networks reported dedicating a section of the agenda to discuss equity-related topics or providing participants an opportunity to discuss, and 16 percent reflected on their identities and how these identities might influence their work in schools. Intermediary staff at a smaller number of net-

FIGURE 3.1
Topics Covered at Network Convenings

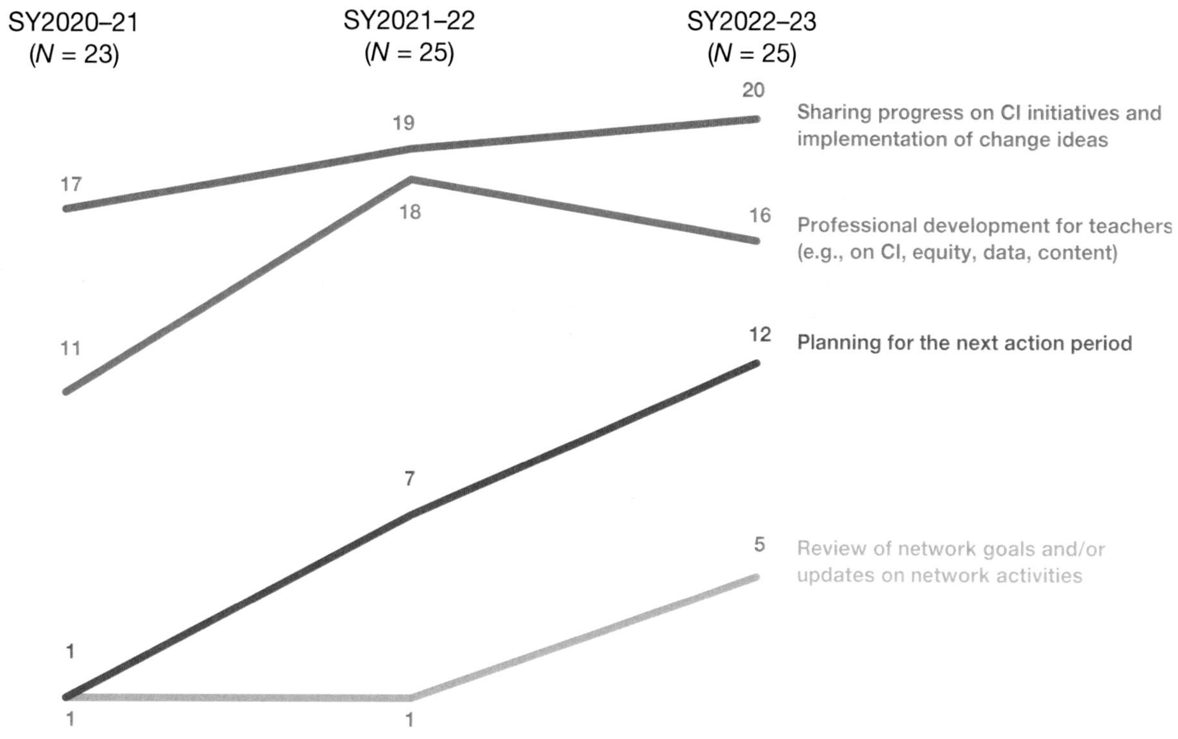

SOURCE: Intermediary staff, interviews with authors, spring/summer of each year of data collection.

works also mentioned having guest experts to speak about equity-related topics (such as addressing the deficit mindset), building equity pauses into convening agendas to get participants comfortable talking about equity issues regularly,[5] and developing a shared network equity statement to help participants understand the equity goals that the network aims to accomplish. All three case study network convenings we observed in spring 2023 addressed equity.[6] Two network convenings integrated equity discussions throughout the agenda, and another reserved a dedicated half-day for equity topics.

Convenings commonly included small-group breakout sessions, spotlights of network schools, and relationship-building exercises; all these strategies grew more common between SY2020–21 and SY2022–23. To promote sharing between network schools, intermediary staff separated network participants into small breakout sessions in the majority of networks (72 percent) in SY2022–23. These breakout sessions were organized either randomly or purposefully (e.g., by staff role, CI focus, or school type) to allow participants from different schools to share experiences with one another. One network participant described the value of paired school sharing as follows:

> [Our network does] breakout rooms where they pair up two schools together and we share what we did in our cycle. It was really, really great to hear and see what other schools did and to get ideas . . . and contact this person if you're interested, . . . trying to keep us connected afterwards, too.

5 An *equity pause* is an equity-focused discussion prompt.

6 We were able to observe only three network convenings in 2023; one case study network canceled its scheduled convening in spring 2023, and the other case study network's convening was an end-of-year celebration party. In 2022, one case study network canceled its convening.

Less than half of networks (44 percent) reported "spotlighting" network schools that had demonstrated progress on implementing a promising CI practice through having the school describe its experience with the network. Roughly one-third of networks (32 percent) included relationship-building exercises (e.g., quick reflection sessions with a partner, book clubs) as part of the convening activities. Intermediary staff noted that these relationship-building strategies helped participants feel comfortable sharing and learning with others at the event; use of this strategy appears to have grown over time. Finally, 64 percent of networks in SY2022–23 (up from 0 percent in SY2020–21) noted that discussing and analyzing data together as a network was both an important topic and a strategy for facilitating learning and sharing at the convenings (see Table 3.5).

School staff in the average network indicated that their fellow network participants share what they have learned across the network, according to the 2022 PNI Network Health Survey. In the average network, staff reported that most network participants share information about what does and does not work (4.01), are usually comfortable talking about problems and disagreements (4.02), and really listen to each other (4.13).[7]

Build and Support School Capacity for CI

Once networks were launched, intermediaries worked directly with CI teams at network schools to develop the schools' capacity to use CI processes. Intermediaries coached CI teams, provided guidance and structure specific to the CI approach, and supported CI teams' use of data.

Coaching to Help Network Participants Build Capacity

First, we discuss how intermediaries provided coaching to help build network participants' capacity, including frequency, types of recipients, topics, and coaching strategies.

Coaching was common and frequent across the networks. Across years, almost all intermediaries (96 percent) provided some form of coaching to network participants, but the coaching recipients and frequency varied across networks.[8] In SY2022–23, more than half of intermediaries (56 percent) provided biweekly coaching; fewer provided weekly coaching (28 percent) or monthly coaching (16 percent). Table 3.6 provides an overview of the frequency of coaching.

TABLE 3.5

Strategies to Promote Sharing and Learning at Network Convenings

Strategy	SY2020–21 (*N* = 23)	SY2021–22 (*N* = 25)	SY2022–23 (*N* = 25)
Breakout groups	11	12	18
Examination of network data together at convenings	0	6	16
Structured protocols	3	5	12
Strategy and innovation spotlights	7	4	11
Relationship-building exercises	3	0	8
CI teamwork time	2	4	8

SOURCE: Intermediary staff, interviews with authors, spring/summer of each year of data collection.

7 Survey responses were rated on a 5-point scale, where 1 = very few, 2 = some, 3 = about half, 4 = most, and 5 = all.

8 One network stopped providing coaching in SY2022–23 because it decided to shift capacity-building resources to other activities; therefore, counts for 2023 coaching activities do not include this network.

Coaches built school-level capacity by increasingly coaching leaders and focusing on leadership and equity. Over time, many intermediaries shifted away from mainly coaching CI teams in SY2020–21 (74 percent of networks) to coaching team leaders in SY2022–23 (76 percent of networks). As shown in Table 3.7, only a few networks coached school leaders, and the number of networks that engaged in the practice declined over the three-year period.

Intermediaries have also adjusted what they coached about, with more networks providing coaching on equity and leadership and fewer on specific change ideas in recent years (see Table 3.8). In SY2022–23, almost all networks (96 percent) provided coaching to participants on building capacity around CI methodologies, which included using Plan-Do-Study-Act (PDSA) cycles and focusing on specific activities (e.g., selecting change ideas). Additionally, all but one network provided coaching on data use. Coaches in roughly two-thirds of networks (68 percent) provided explicit coaching on equity (e.g., guiding teams to consider equity

TABLE 3.6

Coaching Frequency

Frequency	SY2020–21 (*N* = 23)	SY2021–22 (*N* = 25)	SY2022–23 (*N* = 25)
Weekly	7	9	7
Biweekly	9	11	14
Monthly	14	5	4

SOURCE: Intermediary staff, interviews with authors, spring/summer of each year of data collection.

TABLE 3.7

Coaching Recipients

Recipient	SY2020–21 (*N* = 23)	SY2021–22 (*N* = 25)	SY2022–23 (*N* = 25)
CI team	17	12	9
CI team leader	9	14	19
School leader/administrator	7	6	4

SOURCE: Intermediary staff, interviews with authors, spring/summer of each year of data collection.

TABLE 3.8

Topics Covered in Coaching

Topic	SY2020–21 (*N* = 23)	SY2021–22 (*N* = 25)	SY2022–23 (*N* = 25)
CI	21	24	24
Data use	1[a]	23	24
Equity	2[a]	19	17
Leadership	0[a]	14	11
Change idea content	12[a]	5	5

SOURCE: Intermediary staff, interviews with authors, spring/summer of each year of data collection.

[a] In SY2021–22 and SY2022–23, we used a structured intake form to systematically collect these data from intermediaries, whereas in SY2020–21, we relied on topics brought up by respondents in interviews. This may account for the change between SY2020–21 and later years.

implications in their work, reviewing disaggregated data to focus on equity issues for student subpopulations). Network participants generally agreed with intermediaries about the most prevalent coaching topics. On the SY2022–23 Team Connections Survey, the majority of respondents in a network agreed or strongly agreed that their coach improved their ability to implement CI (88 percent), analyzed data to inform their CI work (90 percent), guided their team in analyzing data (90 percent), and raised questions about equity implications (86 percent).

The role of coaches moved from leading to supporting teams. We saw some shifts in coaching roles over the years. First, we used patterns observed across networks in the first years of the study to categorize the role of coaches in working with their networks as either *coach-led* (i.e., coaches plan and lead all meetings), *coach-supported* (i.e., team leaders help facilitate meetings, coaches often provide agenda and resources), or *team-led* (i.e., coaches develop team leaders' capacity to independently facilitate meetings) (see Figure 3.2).

Over the three-year period, we saw a shift away from coach-led approaches and toward more coach-supported and team-led approaches (see Figure 3.3). In SY2022–23, more than half of interviewed networks (56 percent) reported using a coach-supported approach—in which coaches and CI teams or CI team leaders collaboratively designed agendas, activities, and topics for meetings and shared facilitation responsibilities—compared with 35 percent of networks in SY2020–21. In contrast, only one network used a coach-led approach in SY2022–23—in which coaches directly facilitated the CI team meetings, often providing a predetermined agenda, activities, and discussion topics—whereas eight networks (35 percent) used this approach in SY2020–21. Across the study years, roughly one-fourth to one-third of networks used a team-led approach, in which coaches worked with CI team leaders to support their own internal leadership of CI team meetings and activities. These changes over time might reflect a natural progression as schools in the network gain capacity, might reflect learning on the part of the intermediaries, or might relate to external events happening concurrently with NSI implementation. The final report will analyze these possibilities.

Coaches used similar coaching strategies (e.g., reflective questioning, monitoring CI progress, tools and protocols) across networks, and there were no clear patterns of changes over time. Across the study years, intermediary staff reported similar coaching strategies (see Table 3.9). For SY2022–23, the majority of networks reported using reflective questioning (84 percent), monitoring progress on CI initiatives (76 percent), introducing tools and protocols and modeling their uses (72 percent), and observing team meetings or other school meetings to provide feedback (64 percent).

FIGURE 3.2
Three Coaching Approaches

FIGURE 3.3
Coaching Approaches, by Year

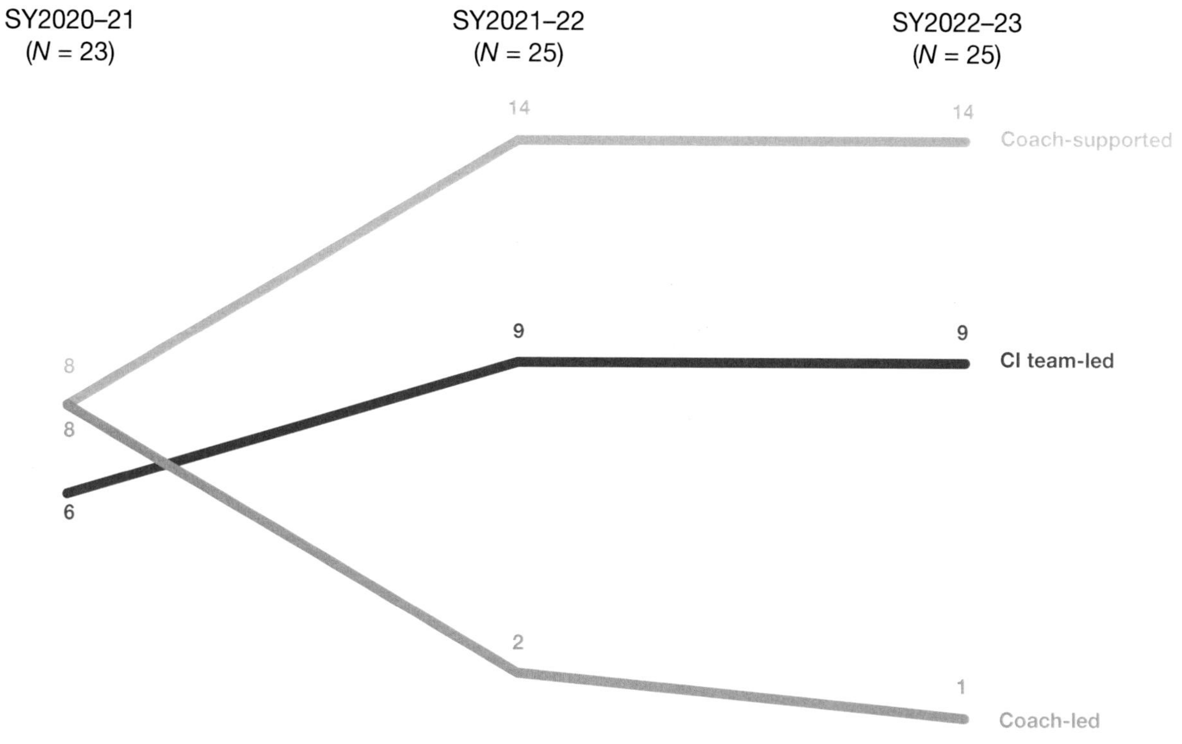

SOURCE: Intermediary staff, interviews with authors, spring/summer of each year of data collection.

TABLE 3.9
Common Strategies for Coaching, by Year

Strategy	SY2020–21 (*N* = 23)	SY2021–22 (*N* = 25)	SY2022–23 (*N* = 25)
Reflective questioning	6	22	21
Monitoring progress	14	16	19
Tools and protocols	20	16	18
Observation and feedback	4	13	16
Joint work	10	17	14
Modeling	11	9	12
Social engagement	7	13	4

SOURCE: Intermediary staff, interviews with authors, spring/summer of each year of data collection.

Coaches in roughly half of networks described strategies to center equity within their coaching. Coaches in more than half of networks (52 percent) described at least one strategy to center equity in their coaching work for SY2022–23. As shown in Table 3.10, coaches most commonly described enhancing awareness of equity in their coaching (40 percent of networks), creating time and space to reflect on equity issues during coaching sessions (40 percent), and providing disaggregated data as part of coaching (36 percent). Coaches aimed to enhance network participants' awareness of equity primarily by encouraging them to con-

TABLE 3.10
Equity Strategies Used in Coaching

Strategy	SY2020–21 (*N* = 23)	SY2021–22 (*N* = 25)	SY2022–23 (*N* = 25)
Enhancing awareness of equity	10	16	10
Providing opportunity to reflect on equity	2	10	10
Providing disaggregated data	0	10	9
Making sense of data	2	5	6
Using equity pauses	3	8	3

SOURCE: Intermediary staff, interviews with authors, spring/summer of each year of data collection.

sider how equity was addressed in their change ideas and how the intended outcomes would lead to more-equitable learning opportunities for students. Coaches also created the time and space to reflect on broader equity issues. One coach explained, "I'll frequently start our meeting with, 'What is an equity challenge you're facing?' or share a resource or a reading, something to anchor us in equity." We describe support on data disaggregation and making sense of data in more detail in the section on providing and supporting use of data.

Additional analysis (not presented in Table 3.10) found that, across the three study years, coaches at 40 percent of networks reported using equity pauses.[9] Example questions used in equity pauses included "Who are we not hearing from/considering?" and "How will this change benefit Black and Latino students and students experiencing poverty?" Often, these questions were formally embedded within data-analysis protocols or PDSA forms to remind teams to discuss these issues.

Given the relational nature of coaching and the potential for variation across coaches, it took time to integrate strategies to promote equity in coaching work. Over time, coaches in more networks reported providing time for participants to reflect on equity (40 percent of networks in SY2022–23, as compared with 9 percent in SY2020–21).

Supporting Network Participants with CI

This section covers the strategies that intermediaries used to promote and support CI work within their networks over SY2021–22 and SY2022–23.[10] Intermediaries described helping CI teams understand and carry out core CI activities (e.g., root cause analysis, change ideas, PDSA cycles, and monitoring of CI implementation), with a focus on identifying strategies for improvement (change ideas), testing and improving them, and spreading the use of effective change ideas, as well as reflecting on the CI process.

More intermediaries shifted to providing change ideas as many also provided less prescriptive guidance in PDSA cycles in SY2022–23 compared with SY2021–22. From SY2021–22 to SY2022–23, networks reported offering more structure around the selection of change ideas and less prescriptive guidance around PDSA cycle procedures. In SY2022–23, more networks (68 percent) provided change idea packages (sets of change ideas and tools to implement them) and encouraged schools to choose one of their change ideas, as compared with the prior year (20 percent). Intermediary staff suggested that the shift to more structure in the selection of change packages was shaped by two factors: (1) intermediaries identified change ideas working

[9] *Equity pauses* is a recently developed tool by equityXdesign (Ortiz Guzman, 2017), which may explain why only a handful of networks initially mentioned having incorporated it in their work.

[10] Data from SY2020–21 were not included because we did not ask specifics about building CI capacity in this year as we did in subsequent years.

well for some schools and wished to suggest these to the network and (2) multiple change ideas across schools proved too complicated to monitor. One intermediary staff member explained,

> This will be the first time we've had a fair, a good amount of confidence in a change package where we were saying, "Hey, we actually think you should do a bunch of the things in here, and many of you already are, and that's where we got the ideas, but the schools that are finding a lot of success in X are doing these things." So, we are much more change-package-forward than we were in previous years.

Over the same period, intermediaries became less prescriptive in their approach to PDSA cycles. Intermediary staff at only 12 percent of networks in SY2022–23 reported providing prescriptive guidance on how teams should implement PDSA cycles, down from 36 percent of networks in SY2021–22. One possible explanation for this reduction is the pushback that some intermediaries received from schools. Intermediary staff reported that network participants found detailed documentation of PDSA cycles time-consuming and unreflective of the context of their schools; they also reported that network participants often did not complete the cycles as prescribed. For instance, one intermediary staff member explained, "Our schools don't find it useful. It doesn't actually frame the work in the way that we feel like we need to. We don't do 'formal' PDSA cycles in the way that people describe them."

Specifically, in SY2022–23, intermediary staff reported providing guidance that network participants should engage in testing change ideas in general rather than focusing on the formal steps in the PDSA cycle. In some ways, the shifts toward increased standardization of supports and decreased prescriptiveness around PDSA cycles may seem contradictory. Across the networks, however, it seemed that both changes were intended to help lessen the burden on local school staff to identify change ideas, find commonalities for sharing change ideas, and undertake frequent inquiry cycles and documentation.

Provide and Support Use of Data

In this section, we present findings on how networks used data to support their CI work.

Networks increased their use of data over time, especially data from students. Intermediary staff reported that they used a variety of data types in SY2022–23 to guide the CI process, with student voice data (feedback directly from students) used most frequently. In an average network, respondents to the 2022 PNI Network Health Survey agreed, but not strongly, that their network collected and reviewed a rich array of qualitative and quantitative data relevant to the problem (3.83).[11] Networks increased their use of all types of data over time (see Figure 3.4). In SY2022–23, all but one network (96 percent) reported using student voice data from surveys and interviews, up from 61 percent of networks in SY2020–21.[12] For example, one intermediary instructed CI teams to survey their students to find out who would like support with their college applications in order to help teams identify the students who would like targeted support.

Networks used data to revise their change ideas, inform the CI process, and track progress against their network goals. All or almost all networks reported using the data they collected to help CI teams revise change ideas (100 percent), inform the CI process (96 percent), and track progress against their network goals (88 percent) in SY2022–23. When asked about helping CI teams come up with change ideas, one interviewee shared, "We want our schools to learn what works for their kids . . . Once we have enough data to say definitely what is or isn't working for different groups of students . . . [we can do that], but we don't have that

[11] Survey responses were rated on a 5-point scale, where 1 = do not agree, 2 = slightly agree, 3 = moderately agree, 4 = agree, and 5 = strongly agree.

[12] The administration of standardized testing in SY2019–20 and SY2020–21 was affected by the COVID-19 pandemic. The lack of available data may explain why fewer networks used test data in SY2020–21.

FIGURE 3.4
Types of Data Used for CI

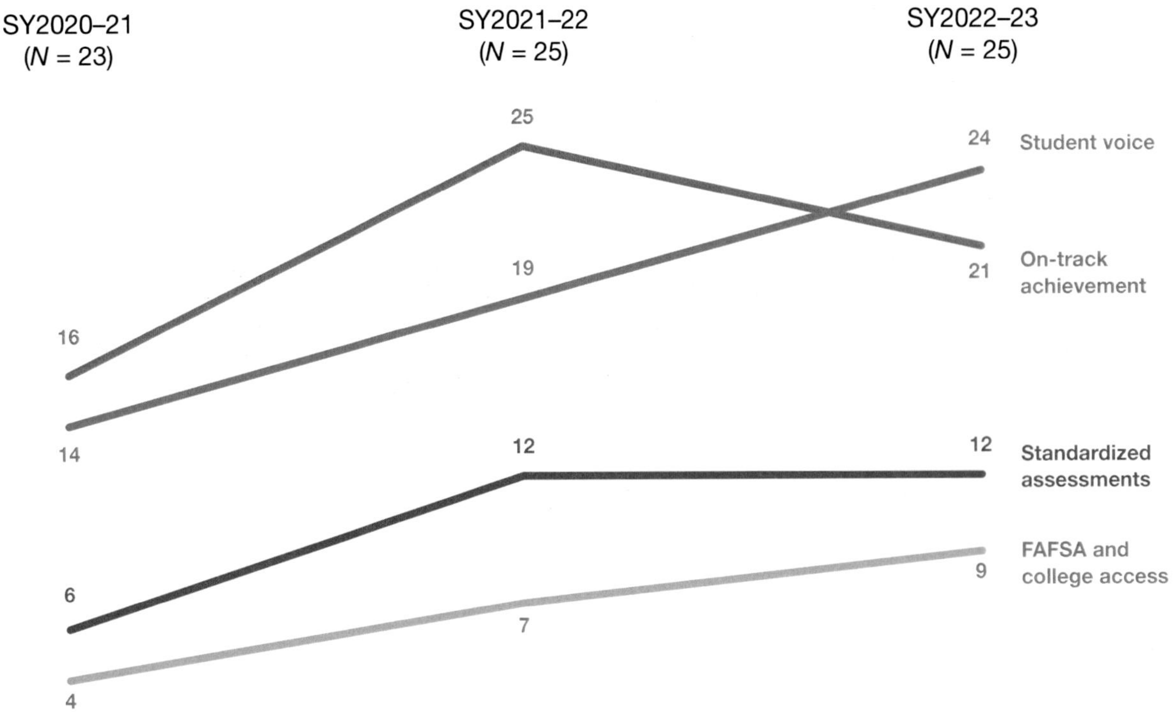

SOURCE: Intermediary staff, interviews with authors, spring/summer of each year of data collection.
NOTE: FAFSA = Free Application for Federal Student Aid.

[data].” About two-thirds of networks in all three years also described using data to assess progress toward network goals. More networks described using data for these purposes over time, as shown in Table 3.11.

School-based CI teams tended to agree—but not strongly—that the data were helpful. In the average network, respondents to the 2022 PNI Network Health Survey agreed that the data helped them understand whether the changes they were making were leading to improvements (3.83).[13] In the average network, respondents also agreed that the data provided useful insights in areas to target for improvement (3.90) and information about their schools and classrooms (3.86) and helped participants understand the reasons for different student outcomes (3.73).

Networks managed and shared data using online platforms, in-person meetings, and snapshots or reports. Most commonly, networks in SY2022–23 used data dashboards (76 percent)—tools to store and present data in useful reports—or convenings (76 percent) to share data, while less than half (44 percent) reported using snapshots or reports (see Table 3.12). More networks in SY2022–23 reported using each tool compared with SY2020–21.

Intermediary staff helped CI teams make sense of their data primarily through meetings or trainings on data analysis, use of data protocols, and PDSA activities. Many intermediary staff members described helping network participants make sense of their data through meetings and trainings to support data processing (96 percent), the use of data protocols (80 percent), and activities related to PDSA cycles (60 percent)

[13] Survey responses were rated on a 5-point scale, where 1 = do not agree, 2 = slightly agree, 3 = moderately agree, 4 = agree, and 5 = strongly agree.

TABLE 3.11
Uses of Data

Use	SY2020–21 (*N* = 23)	SY2021–22 (*N* = 25)	SY2022–23 (*N* = 25)
Tailor change ideas	17	18	25
Inform the CI process	16	21	24
Track network progress	15	22	22

SOURCE: Intermediary staff, interviews with authors, spring/summer of each year of data collection.

TABLE 3.12
Data-Sharing Tools

Tool	SY2020–21 (*N* = 23)	SY2021–22 (*N* = 25)	SY2022–23 (*N* = 25)
Data dashboards	12	17	19
Meetings	9	20	19
Snapshots or reports	5	12	11

SOURCE: Intermediary staff, interviews with authors, spring/summer of each year of data collection.

in SY2022–23. Intermediary staff described data-focused meetings and trainings as crucial to helping network participants better understand and use the information they were getting. One network participant noted how the meetings help people get to their "aha" moments, which they then bring back to their teams. Intermediaries used data protocols to help network participants work with the data systematically and organize data to inform PDSA cycles.

Each year, more networks reported using these strategies to build network participants' capacity to analyze data (see Table 3.13). From SY2020–21 to SY2022–23, an increased share of networks reported using data analysis meetings or trainings (52 percent to 96 percent), data protocols (30 percent to 80 percent), and PDSA activities (22 percent to 60 percent).

Intermediaries reported challenges in using data, such as lack of access to data and discomfort using data. Most interviewed intermediary staff members reported challenges with using data, including a lack of access to data, network participants' discomfort in using data, or data inconsistencies (see Table 3.14). In SY2022–23, roughly two-thirds of networks (64 percent) described difficulty with accessing data (e.g., data are unavailable generally or for key measures, such as socioeconomic status; data are not delivered when expected; software difficulties). Intermediary staff reported this challenge in nearly twice as many networks compared with SY2021–22, suggesting a growing disconnect between a data-based improvement strategy and access to data. Additionally, in both SY2022–23 and SY2021–22, intermediary staff at 60 percent of networks reported that some network participants were not comfortable with using the data (e.g., they were not familiar with certain types of data, or schools in networks had different data). On a positive note, intermediary staff from only 28 percent of networks in SY2022–23 (down from 56 percent in SY2021–22) reported challenges with data inconsistencies.

To center equity in their work with CI teams, networks disaggregated data by student subpopulations, incorporated student voice data, and devoted time to discussing equity. Roughly three-fourths of networks (76 percent) in SY2022–23 reported disaggregating data by student subgroup (e.g., race, family income) to center equity through focusing on specific groups of students. A subset of the networks (48 percent of all

TABLE 3.13

Approaches Used in Building CI Team Capacity to Analyze Data

Approach	SY2020–21 (*N* = 23)	SY2021–22 (*N* = 25)	SY2022–23 (*N* = 25)
Meetings and training on data analysis	12	21	24
Data protocols	7	15	20
PDSA activities	5	15	15

SOURCE: Intermediary staff, interviews with authors, spring/summer of each year of data collection.

TABLE 3.14

Challenges in Data Use

Challenge	SY2020–21 (*N* = 23)	SY2021–22 (*N* = 25)	SY2022–23 (*N* = 25)
Lack of access to data	4[a]	9	16
Discomfort using data	4	15	15
Inconsistent data	5	14	7

SOURCE: Intermediary staff, interviews with authors, spring/summer of each year of data collection.

[a] In SY2020–21, we did not explicitly ask staff whether they had access to data (instead coding responses to general questions about data use), but we did in SY2021–22 and SY2022–23. This may account for the change between SY2020–21 and later years.

networks) who reported using disaggregated data also reported discussing these data with network participants as part of the CI process or coaching conversations in SY2022–23, up from 24 percent in SY2021–22. Intermediary staff described using these conversations to help understand network participants' assumptions; question any existing differences in outcomes; and generate appropriate drivers, theories, and change ideas to help change these outcomes.[14] For example, one intermediary staff member stated,

> So, we developed a schedule of credits protocol—and we broke that data, disaggregated that data into different subgroups, and we had a protocol that—I don't want to say forced—but forced the educators [who are] looking at this data to really look at the data in an equitable way and come up with equitable supports for different groups of students.

The majority of networks (88 percent) in SY2022–23 also reported using student voice data to better understand the unique needs and challenges of their target student populations. On the 2022 PNI Network Health Survey, the average network's participants confirmed that their network uses data to focus on supporting specific students. On average, a network's participants tended to moderately agree or agree that their network studies how the problem is perceived by the target population (i.e., students) closest to it (3.72), that they use data to identify unjust and inequitable practices (3.70), and that their CI process elevates the voices of people who do not typically have power (3.70).[15] Staff at more than twice as many networks reported using either student voice data or disaggregated data to center equity in data in SY2022–23 compared with SY2020–21, as shown in Table 3.15.

[14] Of the schools reporting a connection with their intermediary on the SY2022–23 Team Connections Survey, 82 percent (on average across networks) reported engaging with their intermediary for analyzing data. For individual networks, this response ranged from 50 percent to 100 percent. A *connection* is defined on p. 29 of this report.

[15] Survey responses were rated on a 5-point scale, where 1 = do not agree, 2 = slightly agree, 3 = moderately agree, 4 = agree, and 5 = strongly agree.

TABLE 3.15
Strategies to Promote Equity in Data Use

Strategy	SY2020–21 (*N* = 23)	SY2021–22 (*N* = 25)	SY2022–23 (*N* = 25)
Data disaggregation	9	12	19
Centering student voice/experience	8	18	22

SOURCE: Intermediary staff, interviews with authors, spring/summer of each year of data collection.

Support District–Level Staff

Although the intermediaries largely focused their capacity-building efforts on school-level staff, some also provided support to participating schools' district staff.

The majority of district interviews described receiving supports from intermediaries. The networks focused their efforts on schools rather than the districts housing their schools. However, according to interviews with a subset of districts housing network schools, the majority of district respondents (78 percent) in SY2022–23 reported receiving some support from the intermediaries. Supports included professional development for capacity-building (92 percent) and for content knowledge (75 percent), activities to promote community-building (66 percent), and the provision of tools or resources (66 percent). Additionally, one or two district respondents mentioned having received help from intermediaries on planning, accessing external expertise and resources, or holding districts accountable. One district interviewee described the data analysis provided by their intermediary as "especially useful because [our] data can be compared with other districts [deidentified] so our board can know what progress looks like." Another district interviewee described the value of the intermediary's support to make systematic changes:

> [The intermediary] has actually worked with us to systematically offer district-level supports, convenings, trainings, and coaches for . . . teams. The focus [is] on systems alignment, so working with the [intermediary], we can align with what the [network] is doing systemwide. So, if we are going to improve belonging, make it part of the school's mission and vision . . . [we] drill down what that means and then have a shared understanding of how we are accomplishing that together . . . . Another unique experience has been using the tools that we've learned at the convening to do systems-level work of investigating schoolwide data, not just department data.

In turn, district and school staff were supportive of NSI work. Roughly three-fourths of school-level CI teams (77 percent) in the average network agreed or strongly agreed that staff from their district office actively support or enable NSI work teams, according to the SY2022–23 Team Connections Survey. Furthermore, the majority (89 percent) agreed or strongly agreed that their school leaders actively support or enable NSI work. One district interviewee from SY2022–23 shared that they support the NSI work "by ensuring that participating school teams' [NSI] activities get priority on school/district calendars, celebrating successes by sharing in newsletters and school board meetings, and promoting [NSI] work in walk-throughs with board members."

Crosscutting Analysis on Intermediary Supports for Networks

Center Equity

Earlier sections of this report have described how intermediaries and networks centered equity in pursuit of their NSI goals and the challenges they experienced (summarized in Figure 3.5). This crosscutting section briefly discusses what those practices mean and why they matter for intermediary staff and, ultimately, net-

FIGURE 3.5
Activities to Embed Equity in Intermediary Organization, Network-Building, and School Capacity-Building

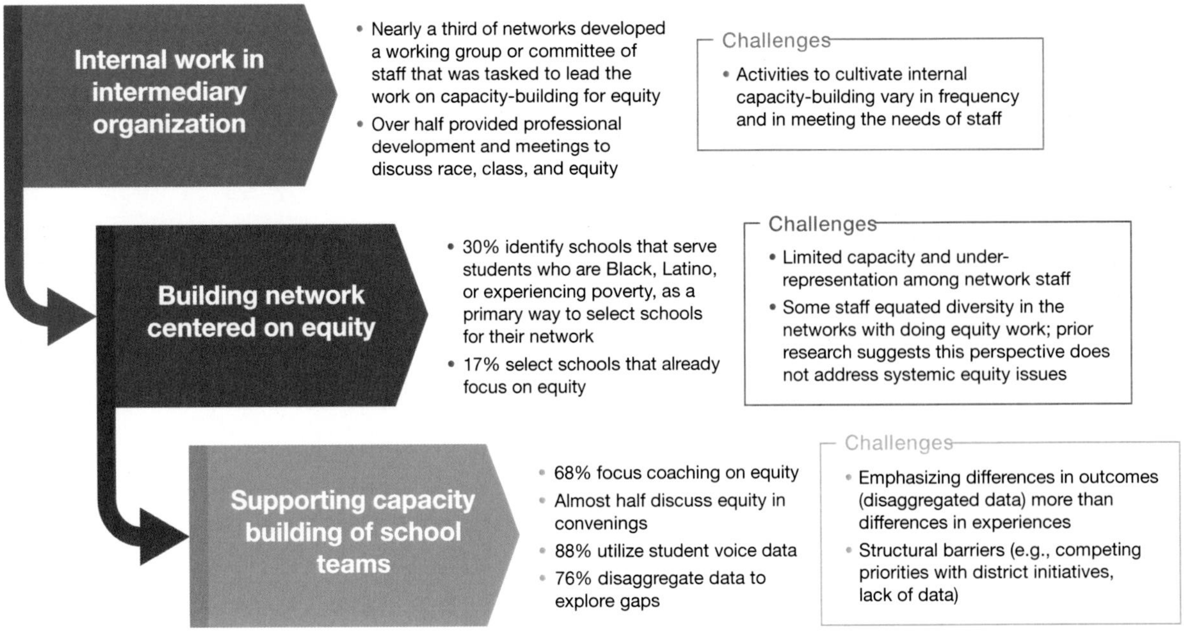

work participants. At the intermediary and network levels, centering equity was about enhancing stakeholders' *equity literacy* or "the cultivation of the skills and consciousness that enable us to recognize, respond to, and redress conditions that deny some students access to educational and other opportunities enjoyed by their peers" (Gorski, 2014).

Intermediaries invested in staff education and embedded equity into core organizational practices to help center equity in their own work. Intermediaries enhanced their knowledge of racial, ethnic, and socioeconomic inequalities and adapted their organizational structure to better center equity in their work through investments in staff education and embedding equity into core organizational practices. Intermediaries changed their organization's staff recruitment and retention practices to focus on diversity and institutionalized the value of equity through new roles and committees and reallocation of responsibilities among staff. Intermediaries also aimed to enhance staff's knowledge of equity vocabulary and concepts through professional development, partnerships with external consultants, and safe dialogues in affinity groups. According to an intermediary staff member,

> We are partnering with an organization that's helping us to dissect ideas around equity that exist throughout the company and also helping us to dissect the identities and experiences that we prioritize in the work that we do. And through that right now we only have a working definition . . . for diversity and equity, and we meet once a month to go through those definitions, share those ideas with our [staff], get that feedback, take it back to the committee, and work through those concepts to develop a more inclusive vision for [the network], and from there we're hoping to extend that into some form of practice.

Despite these efforts, a small handful of intermediaries reported that activities to cultivate internal capacity-building varied in frequency and in meeting the needs of staff. These challenges, while not pervasive, may demonstrate the need for intermediaries to revisit and ensure that their practices are consistently in line with their vision for educational equity.

Intermediaries employed various strategies to help network participants center equity in their school-level work. At the network level, intermediaries employed several strategies to enhance network participants' capacity to center equity in their work. We make sense of these practices by mapping these practices against the Dimensions of Equity framework of access, achievement, and identity (Gutiérrez, 2009).[16] While the framework distinguishes each dimension, there is interconnectedness across all three.

By advancing *access*, we mean priming classroom conditions for students to learn effectively. This includes the availability of supplies (e.g., technology, software), supports (e.g., tutoring), and engaging pedagogies and curriculum, as well as the presence of teachers who are mindful of how their own backgrounds shape their teaching style and knowledgeable of strategies to interact with students in a manner that is affirmative and inclusive. We found that intermediary staff are training network participants to understand students' challenges by using diverse research methods, such as empathy interviews with students and student surveys. In fact, according to a district leader, participating in the NSI has "given us the language and the ideas—for example, empathy interviews . . . that's a very powerful tool. It has changed the mindsets of some of our employees. So, by sitting and taking the time to have those honest conversation[s] with students, we can see that different lens."

The dimension of *achievement* focuses on redressing disparities in student outcomes, especially by building network participants' capacities to gather, organize, and analyze data to help identify patterns of widening or narrowing disparities in student outcomes. For example, intermediaries are building data dashboards to improve access to data and providing training on ways to disaggregate outcomes by subgroups to consider underlying inequalities.

The dimension of *identity* relates to building network participants' capacities to think critically about how their students' racial and ethnic identities and socioeconomic backgrounds matter for their learning and how such reflections can drive participants' NSI work. For instance, some intermediaries encouraged network participants to use evidence-based practices that research has shown to be effective for racially and ethnically minoritized groups or incorporate equity pauses in coaching meetings and convenings to help participants recognize and reflect on their work's implications for their Black and Latino students and students experiencing poverty.

While there is evidence that intermediaries used all three dimensions of equity, they most frequently reported disaggregating student data to identify gaps in achievement and focus their efforts on reducing those gaps. Existing research raises concerns that an overemphasis on student outcomes, rather than on the experience and opportunities provided to Black and Latino students and students experiencing poverty, may not address systemic inequities (Roegman et al., 2018). However, some intermediaries also worked to better understand students' complex identities and how best to engage students as individuals.

In sum, intermediaries started their equity work by building understanding and capacity within their own organization. When they turned to the schools, intermediaries aimed to address a full spectrum of approaches, but current analysis suggests that most intermediaries emphasized one dimension: identifying and redressing gaps in achievement. As intermediaries engaged in efforts to strengthen their equity focus internally, in building their networks, and in supporting capacity-building of school teams, challenges arose in the frequency and usefulness of offerings; limited capacity or misrepresentation; reliance on addressing diversity over equity; emphasis of student outcomes over experience; and structural barriers, such as data access and competing priorities. As intermediaries continue in their work and evolve over time, future analyses will capture the degree to which a focus on achievement is tied to broader, structural changes.

[16] There are four dimensions in the equity framework, including agency. We excluded agency, which emphasizes empowering students to address systemic inequalities because this was not a focus for NSI.

Shifts in Activities over Time

While earlier sections of this report described common patterns in how networks were designed and implemented, here, we briefly describe the notable patterns of change in these activities from SY2020–21 to SY2022–23. As networks are continuing to evolve, this section serves as a preview of how we are exploring network evolution. We plan to share our expanded understanding of network evolution in our final reports in 2026.

Over time, intermediaries are more intentionally embedding equity into their work and building the capacity of CI teams to lead their own CI work. Networks focused more intentionally on embedding equity into their work over time. In SY2020–21, equity was rarely an explicit focus of network goals, even as staff sometimes conceptualized their work as pursuing equity. In subsequent years, networks focused more overtly on equity. Although conceptualizations of equity and the depth of this work varied by network, equity was more often invoked as a primary focus of intermediary and network capacity-building, coaching practice, CI approach, and data analysis in SY2021–22 and SY2022–23 compared with SY2020–21. In the 25 networks that we examined, intermediaries used a variety of approaches to increase discourse and to center equity in professional development training, coaching, and data analysis. These approaches included embedding equity-related reflection questions throughout PDSA cycle procedures and coaching protocols, providing training on identifying implicit biases and deficit-oriented mindsets, and engaging network participants in attending to student voice in their data collection. Nonetheless, the most common way in which networks sought to understand equity was through data disaggregation throughout the study period.

Intermediaries also increasingly sought to build the capacity of CI teams to carry out CI work themselves. For example, coaches tended to shift from directly leading CI teams to supporting school or team leaders in facilitating CI meetings and PDSA cycle progress. At the same time, some intermediaries moved toward more-pragmatic approaches, consonant with what schools could do on their own, accepting rather than pushing capacity limitations. For example, some intermediaries prepared change idea packages for their networks to adopt and adapt. Some intermediaries acknowledged the logistical challenges of documenting PDSA cycles and relaxed requirements for CI teams.

More networks changed their approaches to embedding equity and building capacity between SY2020–21 and SY2021–22; fewer networks made changes the following year. Of note, all of these changes were more pronounced between SY2020–21 and SY2021–22, with less change observed between SY2021–22 and SY2022–23. Each network was at a different stage of implementation in that time—for example, ten networks were in their third year while five were in their fifth year in SY2022–23. We looked to see whether how long a network had been operating (as signaled by grant cohort award year) was driving this pattern; however, we did not observe meaningful differences in change over time by grant cohort. It is possible that events external to the network activities may have influenced the work. For example, because of the loosening of COVID-19 restrictions, many intermediaries moved their convenings from virtual to in-person in SY2022–23, a shift that some interviewees said reduced the frequency of events. Anecdotally, the murder of George Floyd in the summer of 2020 and subsequent focus on racial inequity may have influenced the equity work in the NSI. An alternative explanation is that networks learned from each other and the foundation at the twice-yearly community-of-practice meetings, which may have helped spread practices across NSI participants.

Networks with a focus on instruction may be evolving differently than networks with different focuses. We found some evidence that networks with an instructional focus appear to be evolving differently from those with a different focus, as signaled by network entry points.[17] We compared findings across the three

[17] As noted earlier, the foundation categorized the networks into three entry points based on their aim statements and change ideas: instructional (working to improve the quality of instruction within classrooms), early warning and response (working to create more supportive, connected school environments), and well-matched postsecondary (working to support postsecondary application, enrollment, and persistence).

network entry points: instructional (13 networks), early warning and response (eight networks), and well-matched postsecondary enrollment (four networks). Between SY2021–22 and SY2022–23, there was a large increase in the percentage of early warning and response and well-matched postsecondary networks that created change idea packages and encouraged CI teams to try one of these change ideas (13 percent to 75 percent and 25 percent to 75 percent, respectively). In contrast, the percentage of instructional networks with change idea packages only increased from 31 percent to 54 percent. The smaller proportion of instructional networks offering change idea packages may suggest that instructional changes are more dependent on school or classroom context, while the change ideas in the other entry points (e.g., ideas to promote FAFSA completion in well-matched enrollment networks) could apply more broadly across different schools. In our 2026 report, we hope to be able to better describe the conditions under which networks and intermediaries evolve.

School Teams Engage in Networks and Supports

Throughout the findings reported in the previous sections, we described the supports provided by the intermediaries and the engagement of school teams in those supports. In this section, we focus solely on the engagement of school CI teams with other network members, referred to as *network cohesion*. In our final report, we will also include details about CI teams' levels of participation and how they affect network cohesion.

School improvement networks aim to build connections across network participants in service of the network goals (see Figure 1.2). Networks with higher network cohesion (i.e., networks in which a higher proportion of participants have connections to each other) are associated with higher teacher self-efficacy, greater trust between members, and greater enactment of school reform (Daly et al., 2010; Moolenaar and Sleegers, 2010; Siciliano, 2017). In this section, we share our measures of network cohesion and the network activities that are more commonly used in the most-cohesive networks.

Network cohesion has increased over time; however, most networks lack widespread connections across their networks. We examined three measures of network cohesion from our annual Team Connections Survey: the average percentage of schools within a network that reported connecting to their intermediary, the average percentage of schools within a network that reported connecting to at least one other school in the network, and the average extent to which all network members are connected to all other possible members (density). A *connection* is when a school indicated that it worked with, gave advice to, or received advice from the intermediary or another school in the network. In SY2022–23, 61 percent of schools within a network, on average, reported connecting to their intermediaries (see Table 3.16); networks vary on this measure, with connections to the intermediaries ranging from 40 percent to 80 percent of schools within the network. In SY2022–23, 54 percent of schools in a network, on average, reported connecting to at least one other school in their network; networks' percentage of schools connected to at least one other school ranged from 14 percent to 77 percent. Network density ranged from 3 percent to 53 percent, with an average density of 16 percent; that is, 16 percent of the possible connections among schools in a network were realized.

TABLE 3.16
Average Percentage of Schools Within Networks Reporting Connections

Cohesion Indicator	SY2020–21 (*N* = 15)	SY2021–22 (*N* = 19)	SY2022–23 (*N* = 15)
School connections to intermediary	56	56	61
School connections to another school	39	46	54
Density	13	16	16

SOURCE: Authors' analysis of Team Connections Survey results.

Although these numbers represent an increase compared with SY2020–21, they still are short of widespread connections within networks.

The direction in which guidance flows could indicate both the health of relationships within the network and the gradual accrual of knowledge for network participants. We asked CI team leaders to report, for each relationship, whether they had worked together on shared tasks, provided guidance to others, or received guidance from others. As shown in Table 3.17, we found, on average, that schools were most likely to receive advice from the intermediary and less likely to provide it in SY2022–23. In contrast, schools that participated in the survey were more likely to provide advice to other schools in their network and less likely to receive advice from them.

Network participants, on average, largely agreed that their network is cohesive. On the 2022 PNI Network Health Survey, participants in the average network reported that most of their fellow network participants think that the work is collaborative (4.00) and that their work together is important (4.12). As noted earlier, they also indicated that most peer network participants are working toward a common goal (4.19), are invested in the success of the network as a whole (4.04), and are actively working toward the network's collective success (4.02).[18]

Networks with above-average network cohesion engaged in role-alike meetings, cross-school breakout groups, spotlights of schools, and cross-school visits. Our data suggest that certain activities may correspond to network cohesion (i.e., more connections and exchange of advice, information, or resources). We compared network sharing strategies for the ten networks where at least half of the network's CI team leaders participated in the SY2022–23 Team Connections Survey, divided into two groups: more versus less cohesion.

At first, we looked at network density because prior research has found a positive connection between network density and network performance (Beal et al., 2003; Evans and Dion, 2012) up to a density of approximately 80 percent (Wise, 2014). However, much of the existing research looks at networks of people rather than networks of different organizations or schools, and the relationship between density and network effectiveness is not firmly established for interorganizational networks, such as those in the NSI. In an unpublished 2020 review of the literature on interorganizational networks and network effectiveness, RAND researchers Susan Bush-Mecenas, Karen Christianson, Andrea Prado Tuma, Grace Gahlon, Monica

TABLE 3.17

Average Percentage of Schools Within Networks Sharing, Providing, or Receiving Advice

Directionality of Guidance	SY2020–21 (*N* = 15)	SY2021–22 (*N* = 19)	SY2022–23 (*N* = 15)
Working together with intermediary	91	67	69
Providing advice to intermediary	52	43	55
Receiving advice from intermediary	80	84	72
Working together with school	49	54	52
Providing advice to school	70	44	60
Receiving advice from school	69	41	49

SOURCE: Authors' analysis of Team Connections Survey results.

[18] For both sets of items, response options for the 5-point scale were as follows: 1 = very few, 2 = some, 3 = about half, 4 = most, and 5 = all network members.

Rico, and Ivy Todd found that network effectiveness was linked to two other measures of network cohesion: closeness and centralization. *Closeness* is a measure of how efficiently one organization can be reached by any other organization in the network, and *centralization* is the extent to which network members are connected through a central organization. Because all networks have an intermediary who serves as the central organization in their network, in our second analysis, we then looked at networks where an above-average percentage of schools reported having a connection to the intermediary.

Relative to networks with a lower-than-average percentage of schools reporting a connection to their intermediary, more networks with an above-average percentage of schools reporting a connection with their intermediary ($n = 5$) reported engaging in the following strategies:[19]

- hosting recurring role-alike meetings in addition to convenings
- creating cross-school small groups or pairs for discussion during convenings or meetings
- selecting specific schools to share and present to the network
- facilitating cross-school site visits.

More networks with above-average network density also reported engaging in all of these strategies in SY2022–23. More networks with above-average network density in the SY2020–21, SY2021–22, and SY2022–23 Team Connections Surveys reported using small cross-school discussion groups, relative to networks with below-average density.

Multidistrict networks, compared with single-district networks, engaged in more strategies to promote cross-school learning; on average, they had a higher network density compared with single-district networks. More multidistrict networks than single-district networks engaged in strategies to promote cross-school learning. To promote cross-school learning, a higher percentage of multidistrict networks, as compared with single-district networks, selected specific schools to present to the network (85 percent versus 67 percent), created small cross-site discussion groups (85 percent versus 58 percent), facilitated cross-school visits (38 percent versus 17 percent), and had a knowledge management system to facilitate sharing between schools (46 percent versus 17 percent). Although it might appear that it would be easier to build connections within a single district than across many districts, on average, network density was higher for multidistrict networks (30 percent) than for single-district networks (11 percent) in 2023.

[19] At least 20 percent more networks with an above-average percentage of schools reporting ties to their intermediary reported engaging in these network-sharing strategies.

CHAPTER 4

Conclusion and Implications

In this report, we examined how intermediaries funded through the foundation's NSI initiative designed and implemented their school improvement networks, aimed at improving the educational outcomes for students who are Black, Latino, or experiencing poverty. To this end, we followed 25 networks over the course of three years. We looked at how networks and intermediaries evolved over time and the strategies and contexts that contributed to cohesion.

On the whole, we found commonalities in how intermediaries organized their networks. In recruiting and selecting schools, intermediaries used systematic selection processes and built on their prior relationships with districts to bring schools into their networks.

Almost all intermediaries used coaching to develop network participants' capacity for CI. NSI coaches worked with CI teams initially but shifted over time to mainly coach the CI team leader. Intermediaries also actively supported members in sharing CI strategies across the network, mainly through regular convenings but also through smaller role-alike meetings and knowledge management systems. Networks managed and shared data using online platforms, in-person meetings, and snapshots or reports. Intermediary staff helped CI teams make sense of their data primarily through meetings or trainings on data analysis, use of data protocols, and PDSA activities.

Intermediaries intentionally addressed equity, but there is still room to grow. Intermediaries considered diversity as a factor in recruiting schools. They acknowledged and worked on gaps in their own understanding and approaches. They increasingly helped schools learn from students and use that information to shape improvement efforts. Some networks supported schools in taking a schoolwide approach to equity, such as by developing anti-bias and anti-racist classes or focusing on equitable grading methods. However, NSI mainly addressed equity issues by disaggregating data to identify subgroups that needed additional support—an approach that does not fully address the underlying causes.

In addition to these commonalities in design and implementation, we observed some interesting shifts in how networks evolved over time. Notably, these shifts were more pronounced between SY2020–21 and SY2021–22 than between SY2021–22 and SY2022–23. Although we cannot definitively account for why these shifts occurred, we suggest that intermediaries responded to substantial shifts in context (e.g., the COVID-19 pandemic and its effects on schools, racial justice activism in the wake of the murder of George Floyd).

First, we observed intermediaries' purposeful shift toward discussing, promoting, and pursuing equity as a primary aim in their networks. Indeed, the research literature on CI has increasingly explored the importance of purposefully drawing connections between equity aims and the work of CI (e.g., Bush-Mecenas, 2022; Diamond and Gomez, 2023; Eddy-Spicer and Gomez, 2022). This shift toward centering equity in CI work was reasonable, given world events. The global events of 2020, including the racial justice activism following the murder of George Floyd, brought greater attention to the pursuit of equity, particularly in schools. Despite a significant shift in the focus on equity and evident desire to center equity, determining how to consistently and effectively center equity remains a challenge.

Second, we noted that the majority of networks adopted a more standardized approach to some aspects of CI work and supports over time. This included offering predetermined change idea packages to CI teams for selection and providing agendas, coaching protocols, and other common structures and tools. At the same time, we noted that networks increasingly worked toward increasing ownership of the CI work in CI teams. More and more, coaches supported CI team leaders in leading their own team meetings and activities. Over time, fewer intermediaries provided prescriptive guidance on how to complete PDSA cycles or documented PDSA cycles centrally.

In some ways, the shifts toward increased standardization of supports and local ownership and autonomy might seem contradictory. Across the networks, however, it seemed that standardization functioned to help lessen the burden on local school staff to manage CI work, such that these staff could take on greater ownership. This is consistent with the literature, which has demonstrated the challenges in engaging teachers in the complex and time-consuming work of improvement planning and testing (e.g., Hannan et al., 2015; Sherer et al., 2022; Tichnor-Wagner et al., 2017). Similarly, lessening some prescriptive aspects of PDSA cycles, such as detailed documentation, may be intended to lessen certain burdens on local staff and allow for local adaptation of the CI work. Tension remains between the promise of empowering local practitioners to design and test improvement efforts and the time commitment and capacities that CI work can require of teachers. Knowledge-sharing across the network, in particular, is an area that remained challenging for the networks in our study.

Finally, networks are becoming more cohesive over time. Networks that were especially cohesive appeared to use common strategies: They tended to host recurring role-alike meetings, created cross-school small discussion groups, asked specific schools to present on their work to the rest of the network, and facilitated cross-school site visits. Multidistrict networks were more likely to use these strategies than single-district networks. For our final report, we look forward to exploring the extent to which network cohesion is linked to network outcomes.

Implications

The findings from this interim report hold important implications for a variety of stakeholders, from educators to the research community.

Educators

The increased use of such tools as empathy interviews and student surveys aimed to help network participants (educators) learn more about their students and how both educator and student identities shape their work inside and outside of classrooms. This study has surfaced some ways in which both qualitative and quantitative data contribute to CI implementation. Educators might explore using empathy interviews, student surveys, and similar types of data to better understand the needs of their students.

School and District Leaders

The majority of intermediaries leveraged previous relationships with districts to build out CI in their schools. Although it may be taken for granted that relationships matter, these data demonstrate that cultivation of relationships, communication of expectations, and support throughout the process are important for all those involved. The process of selecting partners via application, the creation of network goals, and the emphasis on equity in building partnerships created dynamic relationships where information and culture appeared to transcend individual intermediaries or individual districts.

School and district leaders might also consider the variety of ways in which NSI members were able to participate in their networks. For example, while convenings are used consistently, small group meetings also appear to contribute to network cohesion. As another example, networks varied in their approaches to and uses of data dashboards, which expanded educators' direct access to data on their students.

Intermediary Staff

Intermediaries were responsible for imparting valuable CI skills and also addressed their own equity needs within their organizations. Intermediaries might consider developing their own organizational capacity to address equity through hiring, organizing staff groups around interests or concerns (affinity groups), and bringing in external partners with equity expertise.

Intermediary staff also provided coaching, which moved from coach-led to team-led over two years. Intermediaries might consider how they can structure their coaching to transition school staff toward local leadership. We note that intermediaries responded to challenges in engaging school staff in CI by modifying or allowing local modification of PDSA cycle procedures. At the same time, intermediaries increasingly offered ready-made change packages for school use and sometimes standardized coaching procedures by providing common agendas, activities, and forms for documentation. These accommodations to pragmatic needs may lead to sustainment of CI practices—or may lead to less meaningful CI implementation. Intermediary staff might consider how to maintain the integrity of the CI process while recognizing the functional needs of the schools they serve.

Research Community

There are several important implications for researchers. This analysis draws on data that were collected over three years from 25 networks and which build on a rich body of case study research. Our findings highlight the commonalities in structures, approaches, strategies, and tools across varied networks. We also describe common challenges, as well as responses to these challenges, across the network. Furthermore, we document varied ways in which intermediaries sought to center equity in their work and in the network activities. We suggest that these topics would benefit from further research to identify the most effective means of adjusting CI practice for use in the school and classroom context and in centering equity in CI work.

Looking Ahead

This report, produced by RAND researchers, on how intermediaries designed and built the NSI is released alongside three other reports: a study of CI processes in NSI schools (produced by AIR), a study of early outcomes of the NSI (produced by Mathematica), and a summary report that brings together these three reports. We encourage readers to take a look at the suite of reports at www.rand.org/nsi.

Our final report on intermediaries and their networks will build on this report. Whereas this report describes the work of intermediaries and their networks three years into the study, the next report, scheduled to be publicly released in 2026, will extend the analysis to cover the full grant period for all cohorts. The additional years of data will help us unpack what is really happening when networks change over time. We will also report on activities of network members after the end of the grant period and intermediary activities that correspond to greater sustainability. Finally, the suite of reports in 2026 will explore the connections among intermediary supports, school use of CI, and, ultimately, student outcomes.

Intermediaries and Networks in the Study Sample

The NSI initiative supports networks of schools in using CI methods to identify and test strategies designed to improve teachers' practices and student supports. Each NSI consisted of an intermediary organization leading a network of about 20 schools (ranging from fewer than ten to more than 50 schools) and supporting teams of school staff in conducting CI. These intermediaries have partnered with almost 800 schools across approximately 150 districts and charter networks to identify, test, refine, and scale strategies to improve students' academic and behavioral outcomes. The foundation funded three cohorts of five-year grants between 2018 and 2020. Most intermediaries leading the NSI are nonprofit education organizations and university-affiliated centers; three are school districts, and one is a charter school network. Table A.1 presents a full list of NSI grantees.

TABLE A.1
Intermediaries and Networks in the Study Sample

Intermediary Name	Network Name[a]	Cohort	Entry Point	Outcome Area	Number of Schools[b]
Access ASU	Arizona Meta Network	2	Well-matched postsecondary	Well-matched postsecondary	24
AIR	Long Beach Network for School Improvement	3	Instructional	8th grade on track	10
Baltimore City Public Schools	9th Grade On Track to Graduate Improvement Network	3	Early warning and response	9th grade on track	12
Baltimore City Public Schools	**Baltimore Secondary Literacy Improvement Community Network**	1	Instructional	8th grade on track; 9th grade on track	25
Bank Street College of Education	Brooklyn South Network for School Improvement	3	Instructional	8th grade on track	11
BARR Center	BARR Network for School Improvement	1B	Early warning and response	College ready on track	30
Connecticut RISE Network	**Connecticut RISE Network**	2	Early warning and response	9th grade on track	9
CORE	Breakthrough Success Community	1	Early warning and response	9th grade on track	24
CORE	Breakthrough Success Community	3	Early warning and response	9th grade on track	11
Denver Public Schools	College Ready on Track Network	1B	Instructional	College ready on track	22
High Tech High Graduate School of Education	CARE Network	3	Instructional	8th grade on track	15
High Tech High Graduate School of Education	CARPE College Access Network	1	Well-matched postsecondary	Well-matched postsecondary	29
New Tech Network	**NTN College Access Network**	1B	Well-matched postsecondary	Well-matched postsecondary	49
New Visions for Public Schools	College Readiness Network for School Improvement	1	Early warning and response	9th grade on track	43
New Visions for Public Schools	**Instructional Network for School Improvement**	3	Instructional	9th grade on track	18
Partners in School Innovation	East Side Alliance Transformation Network	2	Instructional	8th grade on track	7
Partners in School Innovation	Middle Grades Improvement Team Network	2	Instructional	8th grade on track	8

Table A.1—Continued

Intermediary Name	Network Name[a]	Cohort	Entry Point	Outcome Area	Number of Schools[b]
Partners in School Innovation	Middle Grades Success Network	2	Instructional	8th grade on track	8
Partners in School Innovation	On Track for Success Network	2	Instructional	8th grade on track	13
Teach Plus	Teacher-Led Network for School Improvement in Chicago	3	Instructional	8th grade on track	15
Teaching Matters	Teaching Matters Network for School Improvement	3	Instructional	8th grade on track	16
The Commit Partnership	Promise Network for School Improvement	1B	Well-matched postsecondary	Well-matched postsecondary	57
Tulare County Office of Education	**Central Valley Networked Improvement Community: College-Ready**	3	Instructional	College ready on track	14
University of Chicago (UChicago) Network for College Success	Chicago Partner School Network or Network for College Success	1	Early warning and response	9th grade on track	18
UChicago Network for College Success	Freshman Success for Equity Improvement Network	3	Early warning and response	9th grade on track	11

[a] Case study networks are bolded.

[b] As of February 22, 2022.

Abbreviations

AIR	American Institutes for Research
CI	continuous improvement
COVID-19	coronavirus disease 2019
FAFSA	Free Application for Federal Student Aid
NSI	Networks for School Improvement
PDSA	Plan-Do-Study-Act
PNI	Partners for Network Improvement
RQ	research question
SY	school year

Glossary

This glossary provides definitions of key terms pertaining to networks and CI as they are typically used in the NSI initiative.

Change idea. A change idea is a specific practice or intervention that a CI team tests during inquiry cycles. Change ideas are typically designed to meet the goal outlined in the aim statement, focusing on the drivers that guide the network's theory of improvement.

Cohort. A cohort is a group of NSI grants that the Bill & Melinda Gates Foundation awarded around the same time. The foundation awarded the NSI grants in three cohorts: Cohort 1 grants were awarded in 2018, Cohort 1B and 2 grants were awarded in 2019, and Cohort 3 grants were awarded in 2020.

Continuous improvement (CI). CI is a process in which practitioners engage in iterative cycles of inquiry by defining local problems of practice, testing potential change ideas, studying the results, and improving on those change ideas.

Continuous improvement team (CI team). A group of educators that engage in CI (e.g., conduct root cause analysis and disciplined inquiry cycles) to address a local problem of practice.

Drivers. Drivers are factors that influence or produce more-equitable student outcomes. The primary drivers are the major factors thought to lead to improvement. The secondary drivers are the interventions focused on the primary drivers (Bryk, Gomez, and Grunow, 2011). Drivers are often shown as part of a diagram that shows the relationship between the change ideas, drivers, and aims.

Educational equity. Educational equity means providing students with resources, experiences, and environments—allocated based on circumstances and needs—so that students have equal access to opportunities for success. One of the major goals of the NSI initiative is to promote educational equity for Black and Latino students and students experiencing poverty. Intermediaries and the CI teams they support were charged with applying an equity lens to all CI processes, such as the setting of aims and the development of change ideas. The equity framework used for the NSI evaluation consists of four dimensions of equity:

- **Access:** This dimension includes access to teachers who are attentive to student needs (e.g., addressing teacher mindsets), access to supplies (e.g., equipment, software, materials in multiple languages) for effective learning, access to classroom environments that encourage student participation (e.g., perhaps using pedagogical tools that consider how students learn differently), and access to support and opportunity (e.g., tutoring, after-school programs for outside learning).
- **Achievement:** This dimension includes enabling students to achieve traditional outcomes, including grades, test scores, course taking, graduation, and postsecondary attendance, and documenting outcomes and disaggregating data to identify gaps.
- **Identity:** Resources and interventions that are attentive to a student's or teacher's background, which can include personal characteristics, family and community histories, and their membership in social groups based on race, ethnicity, gender, class, status, ability, sexual orientation, religion, language, and many others. Identity situates education as a cultural practice in which learners are able to see themselves and others favorably.
- **Agency:** Resources and interventions that provide students from nondominant backgrounds increased opportunity to use their voices and express agency to challenge contemporary inequalities within and beyond the school walls with the goal of engendering structural change.

Entry point. The foundation categorized the networks into three entry points based on their aim statements and change ideas (Bill & Melinda Gates Foundation, personal correspondence with the authors, June 2021). The entry points are *instructional*, *early warning and response*, and *well-matched postsecondary*. The foundation defines the entry points as follows:

- "**Instructional NSI** work with math or English-language-arts teams within schools, often including instructional coaches, special-education teachers, and English learner/multilingual teachers, to improve the quality of instruction within classrooms."
- "**Early Warning and Response (EWR) NSI** work with grade-level or cross-functional teams within schools to create more supportive school environments, where young people are connected to adults, each other, and the school community."
- "**Well-Matched Postsecondary (WMPS) NSI** work with school-based teams of counselors, service providers, district and school leaders, teachers, and other staff on evidence-based strategies and processes that support postsecondary application, enrollment, and persistence."

Intermediary. An intermediary is an organization that received an NSI grant and is responsible for the facilitation and support of one or more networks and their activities. When multiple organizations work collectively to organize or support the network and its participants, we refer to the collective group as the intermediary.

Inquiry cycles. Inquiry cycles are repeated, iterative tests of change conducted by network participants. Inquiry cycles may be broken into four stages—Plan-Do-Study-Act (PDSA)—that entail the following:

- selecting a change idea and developing a plan that determines how it will be tested (Plan)
- implementing the change idea and collecting relevant data (Do)
- assessing the results based on the collected data (Study)
- using the results to determine whether to adapt, abandon, or adopt the change idea (Act).

Some intermediaries use other conceptualizations of inquiry cycles—for example, Partners for School Innovation bases its work on Results-Oriented Cycles of Inquiry (ROCI). Cycles may have three or five stages, rather than four, or the separate stages may not be clearly defined.

During each cycle, outcomes are compared with predictions, and discrepancies between the two become a major source of learning.

Knowledge management system (KMS). A KMS is a digital platform used to organize, maintain, and share the knowledge, learning, and experiences of NSI participants.

Network. A network is a group that includes a facilitating organization and multiple schools that work together to share knowledge and practice.

Network for School Improvement (NSI). An NSI is a network funded by the Bill & Melinda Gates Foundation. An NSI is a group of intermediary staff and CI teams that work together to share knowledge and practice to produce more-equitable student outcomes. An NSI may contain sub-networks of practitioners based on a variety of factors (e.g., school district, year in which schools entered the network).

On-track threshold. A threshold set by the Bill & Melinda Gates Foundation for each outcome used to measure whether a student is on track to graduate high school and enroll in college. For example, students earning a grade point average (GPA) of 3.0 or higher are considered to be on track with respect to their GPA.

Outcome area. Each intermediary focused its grant on improving student outcomes in one or more of the following areas:

- **8th or 9th grade on track:** The proportion of 8th- or 9th-grade students who meet a set of academic and behavioral outcomes related to high school graduation and college enrollment.
- **College-ready on track:** The proportion of 11th- and 12th-grade students who are on track academically to enroll in a college with a graduation rate of at least 50 percent.
- **Well-matched postsecondary enrollment:** The proportion of 12th-grade students who complete the steps needed to enroll in a college with a high graduation rate (at least 50 percent).

Problem of practice. A problem of practice is a current strategy or practice that network participants have identified as leading to inequitable student outcomes. Network participants address a problem of practice by conducting disciplined inquiry cycles.

Root cause. A root cause is an underlying reason for an educational challenge. Network participants identify root causes to help them understand the systems that produce inequitable outcomes for Black students, Latino students, and students experiencing poverty within their local setting.

Theory of improvement. A theory of improvement includes a set of interrelated hypotheses about how changes in certain practices or policies could lead to improved student outcomes (Carnegie Foundation for the Advancement of Teaching, undated). A theory of improvement guides the work of the network and evolves as educators conduct and learn from inquiry cycles.

References

American Enterprise Institute, "Return 2 Learn Tracker," homepage, undated. As of October 5, 2021:
https://www.returntolearntracker.net

Beal, Daniel J., Robin R. Cohen, Michael J. Burke, and Christy L. McLendon, "Cohesion and Performance in Groups: A Meta-Analytic Clarification of Construct Relations," *Journal of Applied Psychology*, Vol. 88, No. 6, December 2003.

Bryk, Anthony S., Louis M. Gomez, and Alicia Grunow, "Getting Ideas into Action: Building Networked Improvement Communities in Education," in Maureen Hallinan, ed., *Frontiers in Sociology of Education*, Springer, 2011.

Bryk, Anthony S., Louis M. Gomez, Alicia Grunow, and Paul G. LeMahieu, *Learning to Improve: How America's Schools Can Get Better at Getting Better*, Harvard Education Press, 2015.

Bush-Mecenas, Susan, "'The Business of Teaching and Learning': Institutionalizing Equity in Educational Organizations Through Continuous Improvement," *American Educational Research Journal*, Vol. 59, No. 3, February 2022.

Carnegie Foundation for the Advancement of Teaching, "Learning to Improve Glossary," webpage, undated. As of March 5, 2024:
https://www.carnegiefoundation.org/resources/learning-to-improve-glossary

Cattan, Sarah, Daniel A. Kamhöfer, Martin Karlsson, and Therese Nilsson, "The Long-Term Effects of Student Absence: Evidence from Sweden," *Economic Journal*, Vol. 133, No. 650, February 2023.

Chapman, Carrie L., and Danielle M. Varda, "Nonprofit Resource Contribution and Mission Alignment in Interorganizational, Cross-Sector Public Health Networks," *Nonprofit and Voluntary Sector Quarterly*, Vol. 46, No. 5, October 2017.

Daly, Alan J., Nienke M. Moolenaar, Jose M. Bolivar, and Peggy Burke, "Relationships in Reform: The Role of Teachers' Social Networks," *Journal of Educational Administration*, Vol. 48, No. 3, May 2010.

Dee, Thomas S., "Higher Chronic Absenteeism Threatens Academic Recovery from the COVID-19 Pandemic," *Proceedings of the National Academy of Sciences of the United States of America*, Vol. 121, No. 3, January 2024.

Diamond, John B., and Louis M. Gomez, "Disrupting White Supremacy and Anti-Black Racism in Educational Organizations," *Educational Researcher*, March 29, 2023.

DiNicola, Samantha E., Rebecca Herman, and Stephani L. Wrabel, *Evaluation of the Networks for School Improvement Initiative—Networks and Intermediaries: Data Sources and Methodology*, RAND Corporation, RR-A242-2, 2024. As of April 12, 2024:
https://www.rand.org/t/RRA242-2

Eddy-Spicer, David, and Louis M. Gomez, "Accomplishing Meaningful Equity," in Donald J. Peurach, Jennifer Lin Russell, Lora Cohen-Vogel, and William R. Penuel, eds., *The Foundational Handbook on Improvement Research in Education*, Rowman and Littlefield, 2022.

Edelenbos, Jurian, and Erik-Hans Klijn, "Trust in Complex Decision-Making Networks: A Theoretical and Empirical Exploration," *Administration and Society*, Vol. 39, No. 1, March 2007.

Evans, Charles R., and Kenneth L. Dion, "Group Cohesion and Performance: A Meta-Analysis," *Small Group Research*, Vol. 43, No. 6, December 2012.

Fahle, Erin M., Thomas J. Kane, Tyler Patterson, Sean F. Reardon, Douglas O. Staiger, and Elizabeth A. Stuart, "School District and Community Factors Associated with Learning Loss During the COVID-19 Pandemic," Center for Education Policy Research, Harvard University, May 2023.

Feygin, Amy, Liz Nolan, Alexandra Hickling, and Lawrence Friedman, *Evidence for Networked Improvement Communities: A Systematic Review of the Literature*, American Institutes for Research, January 2020.

Garet, Michael S., Sara Mitrano, Ryan Eisner, Julie R. Kochanek, Kathleen T. Jones, Maggi Ibis, and Scott Estrada, "Continuous Improvement in Education Settings: A Literature Review," American Institutes for Research, August 2021.

Goldhaber, Dan, Thomas J. Kane, Andrew McEachin, Emily Morton, Tyler Patterson, and Douglas O. Staiger, *The Consequences of Remote and Hybrid Instruction During the Pandemic*, Center for Education Policy Research, Harvard University, May 2022.

Goldsmith, Stephen, and William D. Eggers, *Governing by Network: The New Shape of the Public Sector*, Brookings Institution Press, 2004.

Gorski, Paul, "Imagining Equity Literacy," *Learning for Justice*, April 10, 2014.

Gutiérrez, Rochelle, "Framing Equity: Helping Students 'Play the Game' and 'Change the Game,'" *Teaching for Excellence and Equity in Mathematics,* Vol. 1, No. 1, Fall 2009.

Hannan, Maggie, Jennifer Lin Russell, Sola Takahashi, and Sandra Park, "Using Improvement Science to Better Support Beginning Teachers: The Case of the Building a Teaching Effectiveness Network," *Journal of Teacher Education*, Vol. 66, No. 5, December 2015.

Jack, Rebecca, Clare Halloran, James Okun, and Emily Oster, "Pandemic Schooling Mode and Student Test Scores: Evidence from U.S. School Districts," *American Economic Review: Insights*, Vol. 5, No. 2, June 2023.

Liu, Jing, Monica Lee, and Seth Gershenson, "The Short- and Long-Run Impacts of Secondary School Absences," *Journal of Public Economics*, Vol. 199, July 2021.

McGuire, Michael, "Collaborative Public Management: Assessing What We Know and How We Know It," *Public Administration Review*, Vol. 66, No. S1, December 2006.

Moolenaar, Nienke M., and Peter J. C. Sleegers, "Social Networks, Trust, and Innovation: The Role of Relationships in Supporting an Innovative Climate in Dutch Schools," in Alan J. Daly, ed., *Social Network Theory and Educational Change*, Harvard Education Press, 2010.

Ortiz Guzman, Christine Marie, *equityXdesign: Leveraging Identity Development in the Creation of an Anti-Racist Equitable Design Thinking Process*, dissertation, Harvard University, April 2017.

Roegman, Rachel, Ala Samarapungavan, Yukiko Maeda, and Gary Johns, "Color-Neutral Disaggregation? Principals' Practices Around Disaggregating Data from Three School Districts," *Educational Administration Quarterly*, Vol. 54, No. 4, October 2018.

Salinas, Cristobal, Jr., "The Complexity of the 'x' in *Latinx*: How Latinx/a/o Students Relate to, Identify with, and Understand the Term *Latinx*," *Journal of Hispanic Higher Education*, Vol. 19, No. 2, April 2020.

Sherer, Jennifer Zoltners, Jennifer Iriti, Jennifer Lin Russell, Rosemary McNelis, Stacy Monosmith, Christopher Matthis, and Courtney Long, *Teacher Participation in an Improvement Network: A Working Paper on Developmental Trajectories*, Nellie Mae Education Foundation, March 2022.

Siciliano, Michael D., "Professional Networks and Street-Level Performance: How Public School Teachers' Advice Networks Influence Student Performance," *American Review of Public Administration*, Vol. 47, No. 1, January 2017.

Thompson, Doris L., and Sherwood Thompson, "Educational Equity and Quality in K-12 Schools: Meeting the Needs of All Students," *Journal for the Advancement of Educational Research International*, Vol. 12, No. 1, Fall 2018.

Tichnor-Wagner, Ariel, John Wachen, Marisa Cannata, and Lora Cohen-Vogel, "Continuous Improvement in the Public School Context: Understanding How Educators Respond to Plan–Do–Study–Act Cycles," *Journal of Educational Change*, Vol. 18, No. 4, November 2017.

U.S. Department of Education, Common Core of Data, database, data for 2017–2018 school year, undated. As of December 1, 2019:
https://nces.ed.gov/ccd/

Wise, Sean, "Can a Team Have Too Much Cohesion? The Dark Side to Network Density," *European Management Journal*, Vol. 32, No. 5, October 2014.